Generosity, Stewardship, and Abundance

Generosity, Stewardship, and Abundance

A Transformational Guide to Church Finance

Lovett H. Weems Jr. and Ann A. Michel

AN ALBAN INSTITUTE BOOK

ROWMAN & LITTLEFIELD
Lanham • Boulder • New York • London

Published by Rowman & Littlefield
An imprint of The Rowman & Littlefield Publishing Group, Inc.
4501 Forbes Boulevard, Suite 200, Lanham, Maryland 20706
www.rowman.com
6 Tinworth Street, London SE11 5AL, United Kingdom

British Library Cataloguing in Publication Information Available

Library of Congress Cataloging-in-Publication Data

Library of Congress Control Number: 2021932751

ISBN: 9781538135327 (cloth : alk. paper)
ISBN: 9781538135334 (pbk. : alk. paper)
ISBN: 9781538135341 (electronic)

♾™ The paper used in this publication meets the minimum requirements of American National Standard for Information Sciences—Permanence of Paper for Printed Library Materials, ANSI/NISO Z39.48-1992.

Contents

Acknowledgments

We are fortunate to work with a gifted and dedicated staff at the Lewis Center for Church Leadership and Wesley Theological Seminary. We especially thank those who assisted with this book. Joe Arnold contributed to the chapter on financial integrity. Carol Follett helped with editing, proofreading, and fact-checking. Matt Lyons helped with charts and graphics. For these coworkers and so many others, we are grateful.

OPENING

Preface

Why another book on stewardship and finance in the church? We both have labored long in the vineyard of stewardship ministry, teaching seminarians, resourcing congregational leaders, and working to sustain the faith institutions dear to our hearts. Our bookshelves groan under the weight of many fine books already published on the subject. For a long time, we assumed we had nothing new to add. But the urgency of the moment has caused us to reconsider.

The plethora of existing literature reflects the reality that every congregation today, no matter how large or small, and every church-related institution is concerned about economic sustainability. This was true when we began writing this book. It is even more true as we complete our manuscript, six months into the COVID-19 pandemic. Moreover, clergy and lay leaders alike are often woefully unprepared for the work of protecting, sustaining, and growing the resources that undergird vital ministry. Our years of work with seminarians, younger clergy, and congregational leaders have revealed an urgent need for basic education on the fundamentals of stewardship and finance.

A GREATER CALLING

Sustaining our faith institutions is critically important, but it is not an end unto itself, as so much of the existing stewardship literature implicitly assumes. God's purpose in calling us to lives of faithful stewardship and generosity isn't merely to sustain the church. In fact, it's the other way around. The continued existence of the church is essential to sustain the powerful, transformative message of our faith regarding how we are to live in relation to money and possessions. Biblical generosity and responsible stewardship are more than a fundraising plan for the church. They are the instruments God uses to counter greed and scarcity, to transform and reconcile communities, and to bring forth the abundant life that God intends for all God's people. They are the means by which God brings forth the kingdom.

In an era of rampant consumerism, unbridled greed, and increasing income inequality across the globe, the world stands in need of the redeeming and transforming power of the Bible's message regarding generosity, stewardship, and abundance. The church has a unique call to inspire responsible and generous living. When the church fulfills this call, generosity spills over to the benefit of the broader community and the world, because people who learn the virtue of generosity in church are most generous beyond the church as well.

God calls the church to responsible stewardship and extravagant generosity not just for our own sake, nor for the sake of our institutions, but for the sake of the world. If the church abdicates this responsibility or is no longer able to fulfill it, no other institution or entity in our world can carry forward this essential gospel call. In short, we don't preach generosity and stewardship merely to sustain the church. We must sustain the church so that we can preach generosity and stewardship for the sake of the world. It is the urgency of this call that compelled us to add yet another title to the corpus of literature on stewardship and finance.

BRIDGING FALSE DICHOTOMIES

This book addresses a wide range of matters related to Christian financial responsibility, bringing together aspects of stewardship that are often treated separately. We integrate the theological and the practical as well as matters of personal and congregational finances under the rubric of three interrelated biblical concepts—generosity, stewardship, and abundance. Our goal is to address money and faith in a holistic and forward-looking way that dispels several false dichotomies.

One of these false dichotomies is the assumption that a spiritual perspective on money requires the abandonment of practical thinking and that a practical perspective is inherently unfaithful. This false notion is too often used to demean or reject the gospel's message about money and possessions. We believe the Christian faith invites people to embrace a worldview regarding money and possessions that is radically different from the dominant worldview in U.S. culture. But the logic of faith is neither naive nor fanciful. We believe that a spiritual perspective regarding money and finances is also a practical perspective, and we do not shy away from discussing tactics and best practices. The book provides down-to-earth advice on encouraging greater giving, building budgets, financing capital needs, and developing new revenue streams to support ministry. Jesus said we must be wise as serpents and innocent as doves. A developmental approach to cultivating giving and adherence to sound financial practices are not accommodations to the world. They are means of transforming the world to the will of God.

Another false dichotomy is the tendency to regard personal stewardship and individual generosity as something separate and apart from congregational stewardship and generosity. To put it crassly, in one realm are matters related to how the church *gets* money and in the other realm are matters of how the church *uses* money. Too often churches preach generosity and abundance when exhorting their members to give but operate out of a mindset of scarcity when managing congregational resources. This book views the calling of individual Christians and the calling of the church regarding stewardship and generosity as holistically interrelated, discussing the two side by side under the rubric of the same theological constructs. Bridging this dichotomy is not merely an academic exercise. Congregations that practice responsible stewardship and extravagant generosity encourage their members to do the same, and vice versa. By the same token, those who fail to see this connection undercut their own efforts.

Finally, we believe the future demands that we have an improved mastery of the basics of stewardship and finance coupled with the ability to think in new, creative ways. We focus on "the basics" while also acknowledging the need to think beyond the basics. In this era of institutional decline, it is no longer adequate merely to do the same things more effectively. Church leaders must be nimble enough to embrace new and innovative approaches while not neglecting the time-tested practices that have sustained congregations for generations.

LEADERSHIP, MONEY, AND MISSION

Although we organized this book within a theological framework, we are neither biblical scholars nor systematic theologians. We are practical theologians focused primarily on the sound exercise of leadership in the church. Writing this book has reminded us of the fundamental connection between leadership and stewardship, two expressions of Christian discipleship that have been at the forefront of our individual and collective work and the work of the Lewis Center for Church Leadership of Wesley Theological Seminary.

As we pulled together our preliminary ideas for this book, we referred to it informally as "The Money Book." Stewardship is about much, much more than money, of course, but our focus is limited to financial stewardship. This *is* a book about money. But as our book took shape, we began to realize that it was even more a book about mission and purpose. Allegiance to God's mission is the consistent subtext running through chapters that address a wide range of subjects: motivating generosity; balancing a budget; building an endowment; and seeking new resources for ministry. Success or failure in all of these hinges on an unrelenting dedication to God's purposes. In this sense, what we offer on the subject of stewardship and finance is an extension of our work in leadership studies.

Church leaders often shy away from hard conversations about money and faith and from difficult decisions related to congregational finances. But avoiding the subject comes at a cost, especially when so many churches seem to be nearing a tipping point. It has been our experience that those willing to step up to the challenging task of leading in the realm of stewardship and finance do so because they love God and are deeply committed to the mission of God's church. Our hope is that this book will inspire such leaders and equip them to teach, preach, and serve so that the gospel of stewardship, generosity, and abundance can transform us, our churches, and God's world.

Chapter 1

The Spirituality of Money

Given the way a lot of church people talk about money, you'd think it is a pretty unholy, disreputable, dangerous thing. They remind us that Jesus threw the money changers out of the temple, that he told the rich ruler that he needed to sell all his possessions to be perfect, that he said it's harder for a rich man to enter the kingdom of God than for a camel to go through the eye of a needle, and that one cannot serve both God and money. This negative attitude often affects how we regard ministries of generosity and financial management. They are at best a necessary evil, but somehow not as pure or admirable or important as other ministries. And sometimes these scriptural admonitions are brandished in ways that deter objective conversations about faith and money.

There *is* much in Scripture to remind us that money can be problematic. It is problematic when we abuse it or hoard it or make it into an idol that detracts from our devotion to God or when it becomes a medium of greed, self-centeredness, and self-aggrandizement. It is also problematic when money becomes an instrument of division or exclusion or when it is used as an excuse for putting some people above others. But taking these cautions seriously does not negate the truth that money can also be used in positive, God-honoring ways to advance the mission of the church and tangibly helps others. Money used properly can be an instrument of God's grace. We must balance the scriptural admonitions against the misuse of money with the biblical examples of financial resources being used to glorify God. Think, for example, of Paul's exhortation to contribute generously for the relief of the Jerusalem church. Think of the generosity of the Israelites in building the tabernacle, or that of Lydia, the prosperous merchant who was a patron of the early church. Ministry takes money. There is no shame in acknowledging that or in working diligently to protect, sustain, and grow the financial resources that support ministry.

The reason Jesus spoke more about money than he did about any subject other than the kingdom of God is not because money is inherently evil. Rather it is because living properly in relation to money is a matter of utmost importance. For individual Christians, the way we use the resources God entrusts to us is a primary way we demonstrate our faith and grow in discipleship. Correspondingly, the proper use of congregational resources is a primary way churches align themselves with God's purposes and propel their missions forward.

MONEY IN PROPER PERSPECTIVE

It's tempting to simplify scriptural teaching on money by plucking a single passage out of context and universalizing its message. In his substantial work *Jesus and Money*, respected New Testament scholar Ben Witherington III argues for a more nuanced, holistic, and contextually informed understanding of faith and money. To counter our tendency to selectively misuse Scripture, Witherington suggests applying three contextual lenses. The first is the canonical context. Scripture is not univocal on matters of money, and we must honor the diversity of biblical perspectives. The second is an understanding of how the economic world of antiquity, based primarily on barter, differed significantly from that of today. "It was entirely possible for an ancient person to be prosperous and well-off while having little or no money at all," writes Witherington. "Money in antiquity was always produced and managed exclusively by the elite members of society. . . . So it is not an accident that almost the only time money comes up in the Jesus tradition is when there is a discussion of some sort of taxes, tolls, or contributions to the temple."[1] Moreover, while the individual is the primary economic actor in free market capitalism, one's livelihood was more communal in biblical times. Third, it is important to understand that the Bible's injunctions regarding wealth are situation-specific. The Book of Proverbs, for example, addresses a social setting of relative prosperity. It matters greatly whether Jesus is speaking to a rich ruler or about a poor widow. The meaning of different teachings must be considered in light of the economic situation of the original audience.

Witherington advances a measured, common sense view of money that does not regard wealth as inherently evil or poverty as a desired state. This nuanced interpretation rejects the notion that the Christian life requires asceticism or the renunciation of all wealth and possessions. But it also requires that we stay on our toes, wary of the potential risks that money can pose to our faithfulness.

ADOPTING A NEW MINDSET

Many people, even people who have been in the church all their lives, struggle with faith's teachings around stewardship and generosity. How do you make sense of the gospel's call to extravagant, sacrificial generosity if you are struggling to make ends meet? What does Jesus's promise of abundant life mean in a world where so many suffer from want, deprivation, and inequality? How can what the Bible teaches about money and giving add up, given what we understand to be the realities of economic life?

This is largely because we are all captive to a cultural mindset regarding money and possessions—a set of assumptions that are so deeply ingrained that we don't realize how much they influence our thinking about what is possible. But the Christian faith invites us to adopt a different mindset based on a different set of economic assumptions and think about what we have, what we need, and what churches can accomplish in new and different ways. This book frames its discussion of individual and congregational stewardship through the lens of three broad theological constructs—generosity, stewardship, and abundance. Each invites us to view matters of money and possessions in ways counter to the dominant cultural narrative. Moving from a cultural to a Christian economic worldview involves several significant mindset shifts.

From Fearfulness to Faith

Our economic system is grounded in a paradigm of fear and risk. We believe it is our responsibility is to protect our own interests. We are taught to always look out for Number One. In contrast, the Christian worldview is grounded in the faith that God will care for us and provide for our needs. This faith is not a naive abdication of prudence in attending to financial matters. But it does release us from anxiety and prevent us from being overly preoccupied with things.

From Scarcity to Abundance

One of the underlying assumptions of a capitalist economy is that goods and services are scarce and must be rationed by means of a market. But faith teaches that our abundant God desires that all God's people be blessed emotionally, spiritually, and materially. Scarcity says there is never enough. Abundance says God has already given us everything we really need. Scarcity says the glass is always half empty. Abundance says our cup is overflowing.

From Acquiring to Giving

Our consumer-driven economy is organized around the premise that individuals are motivated to acquire more and more things. Our possessions are
the ultimate measure of our lives. We believe it is important to "keep up with
the Joneses" and "whoever dies with the most toys wins." In the Christian
faith, ultimate meaning is derived not from what we gain but from what we
give or even sacrifice. In the economy of God, giving is godly, worshipful,
and sacred.

From Obligation to Joy

Our culture says giving is something one does reluctantly. It is at best an obligation, a duty, a form of *noblesse oblige*, a nicety that only the rich can afford.
Bill Gates, Warren Buffett, and Oprah Winfrey can afford to give. But me?
Or my church? We're just getting by. The Christian faith says giving is joyful
response to God's generosity, grace, and love. It is something that we undertake with glad and grateful hearts. Everyone can and should give. God desires
that all people—young or old, rich, or poor—experience the joy of giving.

From Owners to Stewards

One of the bedrock foundations of the American economic system is private
ownership. We possess and control the things that we think are ours. The
attitude is, "I bought it. I paid for it. I deserve it. And it's mine to do with
as I please." In contrast, faith sees things through the lens of stewardship.
Everything belongs to God. We don't truly own anything, not even ourselves.
We are stewards and not owners of the things that God has entrusted to us.

From Secrecy to Transparency

Our culture views income and finances as highly private matters. We're not
comfortable talking about money, often even within our own family. No subject is more private or taboo than how much money someone makes. Why?
Because in our culture money defines our power and worth. And no one
wants to be disclosed as lacking either. Similarly, we jealously guard what we
believe is our prerogative to spend and use money as we see fit. In contrast,
the Christian worldview says that how we regard money and possessions is
part of accountable discipleship lived out in Christian community. The faith
community is expected to talk about money and giving because it is part of
responsible discipleship.

From Transaction to Transformation

The world sees financial matters through the lens of transactional logic. What are the costs and benefits? Is the calculus right? What's the pay off? What's in it for us? Christians too are interested in results. But the logic of faith involves more than a ledger sheet. It rests also on confidence that God will multiply our efforts. It involves transformational thinking not just transactional logic. The Christian is concerned with making a kingdom difference.

At first, these beliefs may seem nonsensical because they defy the world's logic. But as we live into this new mindset, it has the power to transform us and transform the world in which we live. This is because the Christian economic worldview is an embodiment of kingdom logic and the gospel's power to set the world straight by turning our conventional wisdom upside down.

Doubters and scoffers will always dismiss what faith teaches as a nicety we can't always afford. But the economic worldview of faith is not illogical or fanciful simply because it differs from cultural norms. The idea that a faithful approach to finances is inherently impractical is a falsity many use to discredit and undermine what faith teaches. We believe what the Christian faith teaches about money *is* practical. Indeed, it is *very* practical. And in presenting practical teaching on stewardship and finance within a theological framework, we seek to transcend this false dichotomy.

When we understand the importance of money to our faith, we see that ministries of generosity and financial management aren't a necessary evil or a purely pragmatic matter. The work of finance committees and stewardship committees, treasurers and trustees is holy work. It is a calling. It is a ministry that matters to church members seeking to steward their resources faithfully and one that determines a church's ability to fulfill its mission. But this ministry is much more than a fundraising campaign for the local church. When we teach and embody a Christian understanding of money and possessions, we are given an antidote to a culture that extols acquisitiveness, excessive consumerism, and self-interest. It is one of the ways God is at work in the world to bring the world into alignment with God's purposes.

TALKING ABOUT MONEY

In most congregations, there is a conspiracy of silence when it comes to money. It's a taboo subject. Nobody feels comfortable talking about it, and nobody wants to hear about it. Such an attitude is inconsistent with what our faith teaches about money. As individual Christians and participants in Christian congregations, the way we use money is a demonstration of our faith and

values. There is a practical case to be made for frank, open, transparent communication regarding individual giving and how the church receives and uses
money. But there is an even more compelling theological rationale.

There are two principles that, if followed, can change the tone of conversations about money in the church. These principles may seem limiting at
first because of how often we violate them in conventional talk about money.
However, once we begin practicing them, they will become freeing. They will
help us talk more easily about this subject even if we previously dreaded and
have been dissatisfied with our previous attempts.

Principle 1—Never Talk about People's Money Apart from Their Discipleship

Too often, we in the church give the impression that we are most interested
in the portion of money people give to the church. That is not what the Bible
teaches. God is interested in how we use all of our money as well as all other
resources. Our words sometimes imply that we want people to do something
for the church with their money. We do want them to do something with their
money. We want them to glorify God through how they use everything they
have, including their money. The starting point of all money talk should be
the individual's financial situation, not the church's. And the reason to give is
related to their discipleship growth and not the church's needs. There can be
significant preaching and teaching about financial resources but always from
the perspective of people's discipleship.

Principle 2—Never Talk about the Church's Money Apart from Its Mission

Well-meaning people—laity and pastors—seek to encourage giving in strange
ways. They talk about utilities, inflation, insurance, mortgages, repairs, and the
like. But here is the problem with that approach. Not only does it give the impression that our main interest is paying the church's bills but, more importantly, it
communicates a misguided message about why the church exists and how its
money is used. The church is neither in the heating and cooling business nor in
the building maintenance business. We are in the God business. The church only
exists to do God's will. And every dollar that is entrusted to the church can be
used for only one purpose—to fulfill the mission God has for the congregation.
Therefore, there should be no item in the budget that cannot be connected to that
mission. If we cannot show a connection, we do not need that money.

If we always connect any mention of people's money to their discipleship
journey and any talk of the church's money to the church's mission, then we
will help everyone keep their spiritual and financial priorities in order.

SHOULD A PASTOR KNOW WHAT CHURCH MEMBERS GIVE?

Every time we teach a stewardship workshop or class, this question comes up: "Should a pastor have access to contribution records?" This question will inevitably be on the minds of many reading this book. Since it relates to the larger theological question of transparency and accountability regarding money, we address it here. In some congregations, pastors are prohibited from knowing what people contribute. In others, pastors choose to shield themselves from this information. But we believe there are valid theological, pastoral, spiritual, and developmental reasons why pastors, and sometimes other key church leaders, should know what people give.

The stated reason for keeping giving secret often is the concern that a pastor might show favoritism to those who contribute more generously or fail to minister adequately to the less generous. Yet any pastor incapable of ministering fairly and compassionately to someone whose giving isn't up to the mark would probably also play favorites with those who attend worship and Bible study more regularly, too. Yet no one suggests that pastors wear blindfolds in the pulpit to prevent them from seeing who is in the pews on Sunday morning.

Recent research on congregational economic practices found that congregations where clergy had knowledge of individual giving records were more likely than other congregations to have increasing levels of giving.[2] But the more important reasons for knowing what people give are pastoral. A good pastor pays attention to all the signs of spiritual development. And someone's giving is one important fruit of spiritual maturity. Growth in giving can signal a deepening faith commitment. And an unexpected drop in giving can be a symptom of other pastoral concerns, such as illness or unemployment.

Pastors who do not know what people give cannot help but make assumptions. And those assumptions are almost invariably wrong. The quiet shut-in who has not attended church in years might not seem like a key player in the life of your church. But if he or she is the congregation's most faithful tither, doesn't he or she deserve affirmation and thanks? It is easy to assume that an active church leader is also a faithful steward. But what if that leader was never taught the fundamentals of faith and generosity? Isn't it better to know than to guess wrongly?

Despite the valid reasons for pastors and sometimes other key church leaders knowing what people give, money can be a touchy subject. And people might be upset if they assume their giving is unknown to the pastor or others and then find out otherwise. If this information has always been tightly guarded, think carefully about the best ways to begin to pierce the veil of secrecy. Here are a couple of options.

Establish a Policy

Some churches find it helpful to formulate a clear policy around access to giving records. Begin by asking the question, "Who already knows what people give?" Even in churches where there is a high level of secrecy around contributions, *somebody* knows what people give. Is it the teller, the church treasurer, the office bookkeeper, the church administrator, or all of the above? Then ask who else needs to know and why? Do the clergy need to know for pastoral reasons? Do finance or stewardship leaders need to know to promote better stewardship? Formulate a clear policy and ask your finance committee and your governing board to approve it.

Give People an Option

A church in New England had the idea of adding a check box to their pledge card that said, "It is all right to share my pledge amount with my pastor." At the last minute, they decided to make it an opt-out box instead, reading, "Please do not share with my pastor my pledge amount." This alerts people to the fact that the pastor knows but gives them a choice in the matter if it causes discomfort. The pastor reports that very few people check the box.[3]

Leaders Can Model the Way

Ultimately, the best way to foster a culture of greater transparency around giving is to talk about it more. Pastors and other key leaders can model the way by openly discussing how much they give and why. This sharing should be done in thoughtful and appropriate ways, of course. But when we share testimonies about our giving, when we take encouragement rather than offense when someone learns about our generosity, we teach and inspire others about the importance of faithful giving.

We are *not* suggesting that a church share giving amounts from the pulpit or print them in the newsletter. Although strangely, many people who insist on secrecy regarding church giving don't object to their names and giving levels appearing in the annual reports of other charities. In fact, they would be upset if their alma mater or the local hospital left them off their contributors' list! Giving records should be afforded the same level of care and confidentiality as other pastoral matters, available on a need-to-know basis to mature leaders responsible for helping people grow in generosity. Maintaining the conspiracy of silence in churches around money and giving is contrary to responsible stewardship. Accountable discipleship requires that we be far more honest and transparent around everything having to do with faith and money. And being a bit more open about our giving and a little less uptight about who knows are good steps in that direction.

One of a spiritual leader's most important roles is helping others see money and giving through the lens of faith. Leaders play a key role in modeling transparency regarding faith and money. Therefore, the ability to speak about money confidently, frankly, and faithfully is a key leadership competency for pastors and others leading ministries of stewardship and finance. Cultivating this aptitude, including the ability to ask for money in forthright ways, is a key aspect of fruitful leadership for clergy and laity alike.

Part I

GENEROSITY

Chapter 2

Generosity and the Way of God

Our God is a generous, giving God! And *everything* we have—indeed *everything that is*—is a gift from God. This simple yet profound belief is one of three core affirmations shaping how Christians understand our relationship with money and possessions. Our belief in a generous God is so intimately connected to our beliefs about stewardship and abundance that it cannot be understood fully apart from the other two. But generosity is the most convenient starting point for our discussion because God's generosity is something all people of faith, even the youngest of children, intuitively understand. Because we experience it!

The generosity of God is one of the most elemental ways we come to know God's love because God has so graciously bestowed on God's children all good things. The gift of creation. The gift of life itself. The material bounty of the earth. Everything we have is a gift from God! And beyond these material gifts, God also gives us the spiritual gifts of love, faith, grace, forgiveness, and the greatest gift of all—the gift of God's Son, Jesus Christ. "For God so loved the world that he *gave* his only Son" (John 3:16, New Revised Standard Version).[1] Indeed, the whole narrative of Scripture testifies to God's generosity. God's acts in creation, in calling a people, in forming a covenant, in sending Jesus, in calling forth the church, in pouring the Spirit out on us, and in promising us a new creation—these are all acts of generosity. God's very way of being can be summarized as generosity.

Jesus teaches that a God who feeds the sparrows, a God who adorns the lilies of the field, will unfailingly care for us, even more so (Matthew 6:25–34). Faith in God's generosity is not a naive escape from the responsibility of caring for our needs, the needs of our loved ones, or the needs of our churches. Exercising prudence in these matters is part of responsible stewardship. Our assurance that God lovingly and reliably provides for us frees us from anxiety and an unhealthy preoccupation with our own needs.[2]

Yet in a culture that extolls the virtue of self-sufficiency, it can be difficult, especially for successful people, to acknowledge our ultimate dependence on God's provision. Ironically, being of lesser means can make us more aware of how God provides because we know what it means to depend on God for everything. Having ample resources can leave us with the erroneous assumption that we can take care of our own needs, a hubris that blinds us to the ways God provides day by day.

Unfortunately, we may also distort and even abuse the notion of a generous God. We use the truth that everything we have is a gift from God to bolster the untruth that we somehow deserve what we have, or we see material excess as a sign of divine favor. These heresies are at the core of the so-called prosperity gospel. The prosperity gospel teaches that God bestows riches as a reward for faithfulness and it exhorts people to give by teaching "the more you give, the more you get." Scripture and experience do indeed teach that generosity is rewarding. But the rewards do not always come in the form of greater riches. Material wealth is not a divine payoff. Suggesting that the mutual generosity between God and humankind rests on an implicit *quid pro quo* belies the fact that true generosity is motivated by love and sacrifice, not the expectation of receiving something in return.

The truth is we don't deserve anything. God's gifts are unmerited and intended for all. That some have much and others little is not by the design of God. It is most often a consequence of the way humans allocate resources based on greed and self-interest. God does not use generosity as a reward for a faithful few but rather to bring forth abundance for all. In God's economy, generosity is not the cause of inequity. It is the antidote to inequality because generosity counters the greed, hoarding, and scarcity thinking that exacerbate disparity.

When we read Scripture with attentiveness to how generosity functions in the economy of God, we discover that God uses generosity to bring forth abundance and usher in the kingdom. Consider the familiar story of the miracle of the loaves and fishes (John 6:1–14). Sitting with his disciples on a mountainside in Galilee, Jesus sees a large crowd coming toward him and asks his disciple Philip, "Where are we to buy bread for these people to eat?" Philip protests saying even six months' wages couldn't buy bread for such a large crowd. The disciple Andrew sees a boy in the crowd with five barley loaves and two fish. Jesus takes the boy's meager offering, gives thanks, and distributes it. After everyone is fed, there is enough left to fill 12 baskets.

We can imagine that other people arriving on that Galilean hillside brought something to eat. Seeing the crowd, they may have hidden their food because there were operating out of a mindset of scarcity, just as Philip had spoken from a mindset of scarcity. We can also imagine that after seeing Jesus provide for everyone, they may have been willing to share whatever food they had. Why? Because when we believe that God provides, when we believe that there is enough for all, we are inclined to open our hands. The feeding of the 5,000 is a miracle of sharing that begins with the generosity of a boy who gives his food to Jesus. The story illuminates how God uses generosity to overcome scarcity and bring forth abundance.

Consider the familiar parable of the prodigal son (Luke 15:11–32). A father has two sons. The profligate younger son takes his share of the property and squanders it on dissolute living. When he reaches rock bottom, he returns repentant to his father's household asking only to be treated as a hired hand. Instead, the father welcomes him with lavish generosity. He places a robe around his shoulders, a ring on his finger, and sandals on his feet. He calls for music and dancing and killing the fatted calf. These extraordinary gestures of generosity were lavished on a sinner—a lost sheep who had returned to the fold. In this story, generosity is an instrument of God's mercy and grace and inclusiveness.

The parables of the great banquet (Luke 14:15–24) and the laborers in the vineyard (Matthew 20:1–16) are other stories of extreme generosity. In each of these parables, God's generosity is bestowed in unexpected ways—ways that draw into God's household the profligate, the sinner, the outsider, the newcomer, the poor, the blind, and the lame. In these stories, generosity is a means of grace that expands the household of God and extends the kingdom. In each of these stories, God continues to care for the faithful—the older son, the first invited to the banquet, the first hired—but they receive no greater reward. Inclusion in God's household is the very definition of *enough*. We need not covet more or begrudge God's generosity toward others.

GENEROUS PEOPLE

There is an important corollary to our belief in a generous God. Because humankind is created in God's image, we are created to be generous as God is generous. God created us to reflect God's own generosity and to participate in God's generosity. At our very essence, we are designed for giving. It is part of our spiritual DNA. This doesn't mean humankind always acts in generous ways. Sin and greed distort the image of God imprinted on us in the act of creation. We must overcome the lure of selfishness to reflect more perfectly the generosity of our Creator. As we grow in faith and discipleship, we more perfectly reflect the divine image within us.

One way we know we were created for generosity is because giving is so gratifying. In their 2014 book, *The Paradox of Generosity*, sociologists

Christian Smith and Hillary Davidson provide compelling social-scientific evidence demonstrating that generosity leads to a happier, healthier, more purposeful life. They examined a number of generous behaviors, including financial giving, volunteering, relational generosity (giving time, attention, and emotional energy to others), and neighborly generosity (being hospitable and helpful to others). They conclude that all these practices of generosity are positively and significantly associated with five important outcomes—greater personal happiness, physical health, a sense of life purpose, avoidance of depression, and personal growth.[3]

When it comes to giving, our munificent Creator has wired us in ways that promote prosocial, beneficial behaviors—just as babies are programmed to smile and we are programmed to respond. God made generosity gratifying to us because God wants us to be generous. God desires a relationship with human-kind that is one of mutual, reciprocal generosity. God gives to us, and we give back to God in response and in gratitude for what God has given us—in just the same way that any other truly loving relationship involves mutual giving.

But God's purpose in designing us for generosity and calling us to be generous is not merely to deepen our relationship with God or help us to grow in godli-ness, although these fruits are significant. As we grow in generosity, we become instruments of God's purposes in the world. By inviting us to participate in God's generosity, God bestows on us a great privilege—the privilege of being partners in God's redeeming work in the world. We become God's agents in counteracting greed and scarcity and bringing forth the abundance Christ promised.

Sound far-fetched? In their comprehensive study of the giving habits of American Christians, sociologists Christian Smith and Michael Emerson concluded that "if American Christians could somehow find a way to move to practices of reasonably generous giving, they could generate, over and above what they currently give, a total of another $134.4 billion a year."[4] They go on to illustrate how this sum could support a staggering amount of good work in the world from financing ongoing missionary work to feeding and clothing refugee populations around the world, funding a global anti-malaria campaign, supporting 5 million microenterprises, and sponsoring 20 million needy children worldwide through Christian organizations. Their list goes on and on. They conclude that if American Christians were to give from their income generously—not lavishly—but just generously in keeping with the teachings of the faith, "they could transform the world right away."[5]

GENEROUS CHURCH

Just as God created each of us to be generous, God also created the church to reflect and embody divine generosity. Yet too often, we think of the church as the recipient of Christian generosity and not itself an agent of God's generosity. The sad consequence is that most congregations end up spending the lion's share of what is given to them on programs and ministries that benefit their own members, rather than giving beyond themselves.[6]

Congregations that give beyond themselves model, teach, and inspire the generosity they hope to nurture in their members. One Texas church established the ambitious goal of spending 10 percent of their budget in support of new community initiatives. The pastor called it one of the best decisions the church ever made. "We are gaining a reputation in our community as a church that cares and invests in the lives of the broken. The church is excited and vital. We are living out one of our core beliefs—that we can change the world. And, in three years, our giving is up almost 50 percent! . . . It has proven to be one of the best stewardship strategies we have ever adopted. If you want to create a culture of generosity among church members, model generosity as a church."[7] Another church decided to incorporate a tithe to mission as part of an ambitious capital campaign, and many of their donors were inspired to greater generosity because they knew their gifts were supporting more than just building upkeep. For Christians to become generous, they need the help and inspiration of a generous church.

If we are bold enough to claim that people are "giving to God" by placing their treasure in our offering plates, our ecclesiology and our practices must support this assertion. We must embody the call to live and act as the body of Christ. We must embrace the empowering Spirit that God breathed into the church on the day of Pentecost. We must make God's mission our mission. In short, we must fully reflect God's generosity. Anything less risks hypocrisy and invites skepticism.

GENEROSITY FOR THE SAKE OF THE WORLD

God's generosity is so much more than a fundraising plan for the local church. God calls the church to shape people for lives of responsible stewardship and extravagant generosity not just for our own sake, nor for the sake of our institutions, but for the sake of the world. God intends to transform the world through a revolution of generosity, and the church is the training ground. Anyone who does fundraising in secular organizations will tell you that the people who are most generous to their churches are also most generous in support of other good causes. Research on philanthropy confirms that religiously affiliated people give away several times as much money as other Americans. A recent issue of *Philanthropy Magazine* reported that "in study after study, religious practice is the behavioral variable with the strongest and most consistent association with generous giving. And people with religious

motivations don't give just to faith-based causes. They are also much like-
lier than the nonreligious to give to secular causes. Two-thirds of people
who worship at least twice a month give to secular causes, compared to less
than half of non-attenders, and the average secular gift by a church attender
is 20 percent bigger."[8] When churches nurture generosity, it spills over. It
overflows to the benefit of our communities and the world. It has a multiplier
effect because generosity begets generosity.

There is no other institution in our society that has the proclivity, practices,
or perspectives to teach people to put their material resources in proper perspective and inspire generosity. If the church abdicates this responsibility or is
no longer able to fulfill it, no other institution or entity can carry forward this
essential gospel call. In short, the church does not preach and teach generosity merely to sustain itself. Rather, we must sustain the church so that we can
preach and teach generosity for the sake of the world!

PRACTICAL STRATEGIES FOR NURTURING
A CULTURE OF GENEROSITY

Thinking about generosity in such sweeping terms may seem pie-in-the-sky
or impossibly idealistic. But a generous life is made manifest in the realm
of everyday living—in the myriad of daily decisions impacting how we use
resources and relate to others. The church's task in inspiring generosity isn't
merely one of persuasion or education. Like other aspects of faith, generosity
is more often caught than taught. While preaching and teaching are essential
in shaping expectations regarding giving, cultivating generosity is more often
a matter of helping people to learn by doing. The practice of transformative,
biblical generosity is nurtured within a robust culture of generosity reflected
in every aspect of congregational life. Shaping such a culture requires creativity and consistency. Every congregation can take steps to begin to nurture a
culture of generosity.

Use the Offering as a Teaching Moment

Each and every week, the time of offering provides a natural opportunity to
teach the theology of giving and to inspire generosity. What happens during
the collection in your worship service? Is it a joyful, exuberant time? Or is the
plate passed so quickly and quietly that it projects a sense of embarrassment
or distaste? What you speak, sing, and pray during the collection powerfully
shapes your congregation's mindset about giving. Take the opportunity each
week to educate congregants on how offerings are used to the glory of God
by naming specific ministries funded by the church. Prayers dedicating the

offering should communicate a genuine and compelling sense of gratitude and opportunity in our call to give.

Exercise the Vocabulary of Generosity

Congregations with strong cultures of generosity saturate their preaching, prayers, and worship with references to God's generosity, gratitude, and giving as an act of faith. Week in and week out, they use a vocabulary that helps congregants understand the connection between faith and generosity—not just during the offering, not just on Sunday mornings, but using the lens of gratitude and generosity to frame every aspect of congregational life. Building a culture of generosity means finding ways to preach about money, giving, and stewardship throughout the year—not just in the one annual "Stewardship Sermon." Preaching and teaching on stewardship only in conjunction with an annual stewardship appeal allows congregants to dismiss it as mere fundraising. They will be more open to hearing it at other times of the year.

Tell the Story

Congregations with strong cultures of generosity make a point of telling people about the good that comes about as a result of giving. They share success stories. They illustrate how generosity propels their mission. Churches take their givers for granted when they simply assume people understand these connections. Think about all the different ways you might share the good news of how your church uses people's gifts. Newsletter articles. Thank you letters. Testimonies. Mission moments. Social media. YouTube videos. Web postings. And churches that mail out quarterly or annual giving summaries should never let those envelopes drop into the mailbox without including a thank you letter and an attractive one-pager illustrating, "Your Gifts at Work."

Offer Testimonies

People speaking from the heart about why they give and the joy it engenders powerfully shape a culture of generosity. Yet in so many churches, a conspiracy of silence around money blocks this type of witness. Think how much we could learn from one another if we heard from young people and older people, big givers and more modest givers, longtime givers and those just beginning. Think about the possible venues for testimonies besides worship. They could be shared in small groups, in newsletters, or in videos posted to a church website. They could be part of the ongoing life of a church, not just part of a stewardship campaign. Allowing this type of testimony to shape a culture of generosity pierces the veil of secrecy around money and giving by fostering more authentic and transparent conversations. Pastors and other leaders can play a significant role in modeling this type of transparency by sharing their own giving testimonies.

Say Thank You

Gratitude and generosity are two sides of the same coin. Saying thank you promptly and regularly is one of the simplest and most effective things a congregation can do to reinforce a sense of gratitude and enhance giving. When people are thanked regularly, they feel appreciated, valued, and needed—which makes them more likely to support ministry with their time, talents, and financial support. Take stock of the various opportunities you have to express gratitude to your contributors—when someone gives to the church for the first time, when someone makes or fulfills a pledge, when giving statements are mailed out, or when a special gift is made. Then, make a plan for saying thank you in appropriate ways at these various junctures. A well-thought-out thank you system instills gratitude and reinforces generosity.

Teach about Giving during Advent and Christmas

Because holiday gift-giving is so deeply engrained in secular culture, Christmas is a logical time for the church to teach about generosity. Some churches have adopted the slogan "Christmas is not your birthday"[9] and challenge families to give to worthy causes the equivalent of what they spend on one another. Other churches give all the offerings received at Christmas to a cause beyond their church. This models generosity and demonstrates the church's commitment to mission. At Christmastime, the church also has an obligation to help people see the lure of consumerism and point them to more genuine expressions of love and generosity.

Involve Children and Youth

If a toddler has ever crammed a soggy Cheerio into your mouth, you know that even babies are wired for generosity. Children of all ages understand the simple message that we have received much from God and God wants us to be generous in return. Emphasizing generosity in ministry with children not only prepares a future generation of givers, but it helps form parents and families as well because adults often pay extra attention to what their children are taught. The same is true for youth. When youth are responsible for raising funds to support their own programs and mission activities, it builds a sense of ownership and gets others enthused about giving. Make sure children and youth are given the opportunity to participate in the offering in a meaningful and appropriate way. And remind parents that their participation in the offering is a teachable moment for their children.

THE GRACIOUS INVITATION OF GENEROSITY

In many churches, the conversation around money and giving relies heavily on the vocabulary of stewardship and tithing. Stewardship and tithing are, of course, important elements of a biblical theology of giving. But fewer and fewer people begin their journey of generosity with a full understanding of these terms. Too often they are heard as thinly veiled euphemisms for church fundraising or finger-wagging legalisms, in part because that's the way we have allowed them to be used.

The Christian faith tells a wonderful, hopeful, inspiring story of a generous God who calls us to be generous. The language of generosity is a simple, relatable way to talk about the importance of giving. Putting our initial emphasis on generosity does not diminish our responsibility as stewards nor detract from the challenge of tithing. Rather, it helps us see stewardship and tithing as connected to a larger theological construct—the generosity of God. Stewardship and tithing become more important and more inspiring when they are part of the larger call to partner, through our generosity, in God's work in the world.

Chapter 3

What Faith Teaches about Giving

Wouldn't it be great if people entered our church doors saying "I'm so glad I've found this church! Where do I sign up to give my 10 percent?" In previous generations, perhaps some people did, including those who grew up in the church and had giving and tithing modeled for them from an early age. But fewer people in our culture, even those within our churches, have been taught the normative expectations of the faith regarding giving. Some are not only ignorant, they are also hostile. Their defenses go up at the slightest mention of money or giving, because they have been conditioned to expect that the church is after their money.

Today, attitudes about money, possessions, and giving are far more likely to be shaped by secular culture than by what the Bible teaches, even for many who regularly sit in our pews. So, the church must be far more intentional in teaching people to give. Fully embracing the call to Christian generosity is a matter of faith formation and discipleship growth that occurs over a lifetime. It is caught more than taught. But understanding the basics of what faith and scripture teach about giving are guideposts on that journey.

In *Preaching and Stewardship*, Craig Satterlee suggests that several key questions are critical in addressing matters of stewardship and giving, including these three basic questions: Why do we give? How do we give? How much do we give?[1] These questions provide a simple framework for summarizing what Scripture and tradition teach about a Christian's call to give. There is a deeper logic embedded in this sequence of questions. As people travel the road from new giver toward joyful, sacrificial generosity, each of these questions is relevant at a different stage in the journey. For someone at the starting line, "Why do I give?" is the most relevant question. As that person ventures down the path of growth in faith and generosity, "How do I give?" becomes the relevant question. Finally, as a giver approaches maturity as a disciple and steward, the question "How much do I give?" becomes most relevant. Too often, conversations about giving jump immediately to "How much?" and short circuit the earlier questions that lay the groundwork for this consideration. How can we logically expect someone to give away a sacrificial portion of what they have if they don't yet understand why faith calls them to give? As people mature as givers, it is important to address why, how, and how much in turn.

WHY DO WE GIVE?

A lot of giving appeals start from the premise that the purpose of a Christian's giving is to finance the church. Asking people to give to support institutional needs may resonate with a segment of people already intensely loyal to the institution. But among younger generations, fewer and fewer are motivated by such institutional imperatives. Christians certainly need to be mindful of the church's needs. But ultimately, our reason for giving isn't just to pay the bills or balance the budget. Faithful Christian giving is not primarily about the institution's need to receive. It is about the giver's need to give. It is grounded in spiritual rather than secular logic. Giving that is an intrinsic expression of our faith is more satisfying to the giver, more pleasing to God, and ultimately more likely to be adequate in relation to the church's needs. What then does our faith teach about why we are to give?

We Give in Gratitude for What God Has Given Us

The most fundamental rationale for Christian giving flows directly from our belief in God's generosity. Acknowledging God as the source of all we have inspires a deep gratitude that motivates us to give back to God and to others not out of obligation but out of love. Mutual, reciprocal generosity is part of any loving relationship. Such is the nature of the relationship between God and humankind. God gives to us and we give to God. "What shall I return to the Lord for all his bounty to me? . . . I will offer to you a thanksgiving sacrifice and call on the name of the Lord" (Psalm 116:12, 17).

We Give as an Act of Worship

How did our spiritual ancestors worship God? The ancient Israelites worshipped by bringing sacrifices of livestock, grain, wine, and incense to the altar of God. These gifts were tangible, meaningful expressions of their devotion to God because these commodities were essential to their livelihood. It's easy to give away something of no consequence. But when we give something we labor for and depend on, it is a meaningful sacrifice, a meaningful form of worship. As the Israelite system of worship developed, people realized that, rather than just pouring out or burning up these offerings, they could be used to pay priests or feed the poor. It was a good idea, but it was not the primary reason for making the offering. Mark Allan Powell reminds us that "the point was not what happened to the grain after it was placed on the altar; the point was simply putting that grain on the altar in the first place."[2]

We no longer worship God with sacrifices of grain and livestock. But for modern people, our monetary gifts are tangible, meaningful expressions of our devotion to God, just as grain and livestock were in Old Testament times, because they represent a meaningful, tangible sacrifice of what is essential to our livelihood. In this sense, giving is the most ancient and elemental act of worship. We easily lose sight of the deep spiritual significance of giving as an act of worship. We can't blame the people in our pews for thinking their gifts to the church are a transaction, the price of admission, a way of paying for what the church offers. We can't blame them because that's often how church leaders talk about it. But our spiritual heritage calls us to reclaim worship as the fundamental purpose of giving.

What would it mean to take seriously the idea that offerings are our most fundamental form of worship? A form of sacrifice that is pleasing to God? Writing a check, placing bills or coins in an offering envelope, donating through a website—these ways of giving aren't quite as dramatic as entering the temple with a live goat or dove. Our ways of giving are so discrete, tidy, and virtually invisible that it's easy to lose sight of the connection between giving and worship. So, we must work harder and be more creative in rebuilding this essential foundation of our theology of giving. An offering should be part of *every* service of worship, even if people are dedicating gifts made electronically or mailed monthly. Above all, we must consistently name and frame why our offerings are an essential form of worship and praise.

We Give to Bear Witness to Our Faith

There is an old adage that says, "If you want to know what's really important to a person, look at their checkbook or their calendar." How we spend our money and our time is the ultimate expression of our values because it gives tangible witness to what we hold most dear. It's where the rubber hits the road in our journey of discipleship.

As a parent, I (Ann) knew my children were watching when I took money out of my pocketbook, sealed it in an offering envelope, and placed it in the offering plate each Sunday. One week, one of my sons said, "Mom, that's a lot of money. Do you give that much each week?" It couldn't have been a more teachable moment. My children are grown and moved away, but I know

others may be influenced by how they see me and other church leaders participate in the offering. The tradition in many African, African American,
and Afro-Caribbean churches of calling tithers forward during the offering
speaks powerfully of the importance of setting an example in giving. If you
give electronically or by mail, great! There are lots of good reasons why you
should that are explored later in this book. But don't waive the offering plate
by. If your church provides a token or card for electronic givers to put in the
basket, use it. Or write on an offering envelope that you gave electronically.
Or make a small additional gift as a token.

But what of this scriptural admonition? "Beware of practicing your piety
before others in order to be seen by them; for then you have no reward from
your Father in heaven. So, whenever you give alms, do not sound a trumpet
before you, as the hypocrites do in the synagogues and in the streets, so that
they may be praised by others. Truly I tell you, they have received their
reward. But when you give alms, do not let your left hand know what your
right hand is doing, so that your alms may be done in secret; and your Father
who sees in secret will reward you" (Matthew 6:1–4).

This teaching addresses the motivation for giving. It warns us against giving for hypocritical reasons, merely to parade our piety or receive praise. Giving in such a manner is an ineffective, counterproductive witness. But giving
faithfully and for the right reasons is a testament to our faith, as it was for
the poor widow who gave two small copper coins. Jesus did not chide her for
making her gift in public as he sat watching across from the temple treasury.
He praised her devotion and sacrifice. Generation after generation have been
inspired by her witness of generosity (Mark 12:41–44).

We Give as a Spiritual Discipline

Like prayer, scripture reading, fasting, or dedication to service, the practice of
giving regularly and intentionally helps us grow in faith and mature spiritually. It serves as a continual reminder of God's claim on our lives. It requires
us to put our own needs and wants into proper perspective, to set aside our
own interests for the sake of God and others.

Jesus said, "Where your treasure is, there will your heart be also" (Matthew
6:21). People commonly take this to mean we should invest our resources in
what's important to us. But the meaning is just the opposite. Jesus is telling us
that things become important to us when we invest money in them. Think, for
instance, of the difference between renting a car and owning a car. Someone
who rents a car may not give a second thought to its next oil change or the
lifespan of the tires. But someone who buys a car has made an investment and
attends to its long-term maintenance. Jesus tells us if we put our money where

we want our heart to rest, then our heart will follow. If we want our heart to be with God, we need to invest in the mission of God.[3]

To give something away is a profound act of faith. It says "I believe I have enough. I believe that God will continue to provide for me." Every time we exercise generosity, we step out on those faith claims. And as we flex the muscle of that faith, our faith grows stronger. Generosity is a fruit of the Spirit. It is a tool God uses to shape our hearts. And through the spiritual discipline of giving, our hearts become one with God's heart and our faith grows.

We Give to Counter Our Tendencies to Greed and Self-Centeredness

In our consumerist culture, we are bombarded, almost from the moment we are born, with advertisements and other cultural messages that condition us to want and spend more and more. We come to believe our lives are measured by what we buy and have. Do we wear the latest fashions? Drive the hottest car? Use the most recent technological gadgets? Live in the most desirable neighborhood? In our heart of hearts, we know these things don't define our value. And yet we constantly succumb to the lure of consumerism because it plays on our greed and insecurity.

When sociologists Christian Smith and Michael Emerson set out to explain why so few Christians are giving up to the standards of their faith, the first hypothesis they tested was that people couldn't afford to give generously—what they call "resource constraint." But they quickly rejected this hypothesis largely based on consumer spending data that revealed massive discretionary spending an everything from candy and snack foods to entertainment, technology, jewelry, luxury goods, larger and larger homes, and so on. Smith and Emerson concluded that if people don't have enough money to give, it is less a matter of financial capacity and more a matter of spending priorities.[4] The more salient factor keeping Christians from giving, they concluded, is not resource constraint but rather "subjective resource constraint."[5] It's not that people *can't* afford to give, but that they *think* they can't afford to give because they are caught in a spending trap fueled by glittering media images, the constant barrage of advertisements, and residential patterns that shield middle- and upper-income people from those who are less well-off. The result is that most Americans, even among the upper-middle class, see themselves as "just getting by" when by any objective standard they are quite affluent.[6]

If stingy giving is a symptom of "affluenza," what is the cure? Disciplined generosity is God's prescription for overcoming greed. Proportional giving and tithing are tools God gives us to restrain spending on ourselves, to rein in our greed and overconsumption, and to resist the social pressure to want, buy, and have more and more things. Giving is a form of disciplined self-denial that curbs the power of mammon to corrupt our values.[7]

We Give to Participate in God's Mission

Because generosity is an instrument that God uses to bring forth the kingdom and because we are created to be generous as God is generous, giving makes us agents of divine purpose and partners in God's mission. Supporting the good work of the church is part of this call, but it doesn't end at the threshold of the church. The church is the learning laboratory where God apprentices us as agents in the transformation of the world. The call to generosity is a form of spiritual empowerment which unites us with God's purposes. Giving isn't a mundane institutional obligation, but an awesome privilege. The New Testament churches in Macedonia begged earnestly for the privilege of sharing in the ministry to the saints (2 Corinthians 8:4). Still today, the awesome privilege of sharing in God's mission is perhaps our most powerful motivation to give.

HOW DO WE GIVE?

Faith's teachings about how we give are closely related to the reasons why we give. They help us move from intention to action in ways that make manifest our motivations for giving.

We Give Joyfully

Years ago, a television commercial for the American Red Cross depicted a boxer in the corner of the ring, bruised and bloodied, saying "Give until it hurts." When it comes to Christian generosity, a more appropriate slogan might be "Give until it feels really good." While sacrifice and self-denial are part of Christian generosity, we sacrifice gladly, trusting that God redeems our sacrifice to bring forth hope and joy. Many consider giving to the church or other causes a duty or an obligation, something that is done reluctantly or even sometimes under duress. Instead, our faith frees us to give cheerfully, not begrudgingly or out of guilt. It invites us to give with glad and generous hearts in joyful response to God's abundance and grace. As the Apostle Paul taught, "Each of you must give as you have made up your mind, not reluctantly or under compulsion, for God loves a cheerful giver" (2 Corinthians 9:7). Genuine joy in giving is a radiant, contagious, powerful witness.

We Give Purposefully

Many people give impulsively or in a haphazard way—when the mood seizes them, when they happen to get around to it, or when they occasionally show up for Sunday services. There is nothing wrong with making a spontaneous gift when the Spirit lays a claim on your heart. In fact, that's a good thing. But such giving should not take the place of a consistent and deliberate pattern of giving. An intentional approach to giving serves as a continual reminder of God's claim on our lives. It makes us better stewards of our resources. It helps us check our wants and desires. And it makes us more mindful of the needs of others. The quality of purposefulness makes giving a profound spiritual practice that shapes our hearts. Research indicates that when our giving becomes more planned and routinized we become substantially more generous.[8]

Intentionality is central in Paul's teachings about giving in his letters to the Corinthians. Paul writes, "Now concerning the collection for the saints: . . . On the first day of every week, each of you is to put aside and save whatever extra you earn, so that collections need not be taken when I come" (1 Corinthians 16:2). He later writes, "Each of you must give as you have made up your mind" (2 Corinthians 9:7). Faithful giving requires planning, which is part of good stewardship.

We Give First Fruits

One of the religious commands Moses presents to the people in Exodus is, "You shall not delay to make offerings from the fullness of your harvest and from the outflow or your presses. The firstborn of your sons you shall give to me. You shall do the same with your oxen and with your sheep. . . . The choicest of the first fruits of your ground you shall bring into the house of the Lord your God" (Exodus 22:29–30, 23:19). And in gratitude for their deliverance to the Promised Land, the people are commanded to "take some of the first of all the fruit of the ground, which you harvest from the land that the Lord your God is giving you, and you shall put it in a basket and go to the place that the Lord your God will choose as a dwelling for his name" (Deuteronomy 26:2).

Today, many of us think about giving only after all other claims on our resources are satisfied. We give essentially out of our leftovers—that is, if anything is left over with all the pressure to buy, spend, and overextend ourselves financially. First fruits-giving invites us to give off the top, to make giving the first claim on our resources rather than the last, and let other expenditures fall in place in light of that priority. It means offering our best to God, making giving a priority rather than an afterthought.

We Give in Proportion to What We Have

If we give in gratitude for what God has given us, it follows that we should give in proportion to what we have received. In Deuteronomy, the people are commanded as part of the celebration of the festival of weeks to contribute a freewill offering "in proportion to the blessing that you have received from the Lord your God" (Deuteronomy 16:10). And Paul commends the churches of Macedonia for giving "according to their means, and even beyond their means" (2 Corinthians 8:3).

Proportionate giving levels the playing fields. As Craig Satterlee points out, "For those without significant financial resources, proportionate giving is comforting. They know that, from Jesus's perspective, their small gift is incredibly generous. At the same time, those with financial resources cannot take pride in the size of their gifts when their gifts are large in dollar amount but small in terms of percentage."[9] A gift is acceptable, according to Paul, in accordance with what one has, not in accordance with what one does not have (2 Corinthians 8:12).

It seems so logical that those with more should give more. One might assume it happens quite naturally. Sadly, that is not the case. Smith and Emerson found that those with greater capacity to give generally do not maintain higher levels of financial giving. In fact, as people earn more, the percentage of income given to religious organizations decreases.[10]

Tithing is, of course, an expression of the principle of proportionate giving. But before considering what percentage should be given, one must first accept the premise that we are called to give in proportion to what we have. Once someone has adopted the principle of proportionate giving, they can step up toward tithing, even if they start with a much smaller percentage. For some people, the concept of proportionate giving may lead them even beyond tithing. In either case, the principle of proportionality is more important than the percentage.

HOW MUCH DO WE GIVE?

For some, the question "How much we should give?" automatically evokes the answer "a tithe." Tithing is a loaded subject, it seems. Some are convinced that it is God's immutable law. Some attest to the blessings associated with the practice of tithing, while others feel beaten, abused, and belittled by congregations or pastors that project a sense that tithing is the only measure of faith that matters. In other quarters of the church, the term has been divested of its original meaning. Churchgoers so often hear the terms "tithes and offerings" spoken in the same breath that they mistakenly think the terms are synonymous—that tithing is just another word for making an offering. (For clarity's sake, the literal definition of a tithe is a tenth, or 10 percent, and any time the term is used in this book, the meaning is 10 percent.) Amid this confusion and anxiety, it's tempting to simply ignore the subject. But what then when a parishioner or a prospective member asks, "Are Christians required to give 10 percent?" And if not 10 percent, then how much?

The practice of tithing is deeply rooted in Hebrew Scripture. Melchizedek, the priest king of Salem, blesses Abram (later, Abraham) in the name of God Most High. In response, Abram gives Melchizedek a tenth of everything (Genesis 14:17–24). Jacob pledges one-tenth of what he has to God after he dreamed about a ladder between Earth and Heaven and about receiving the presence and blessing of God (Genesis 28:20–22). Through Moses, God instructs the priests about the tithes of the Israelites. "All tithes from the land, whether the seed from the ground or the fruit from the tree, are the Lord's; they are holy to the Lord. . . . All tithes of heard and flock, every tenth one that passes under the shepherd's staff, shall be holy to the Lord" (Leviticus 27: 30, 32). There are, in fact, more references to tithing in the Old Testament than there are to the afterlife.[11]

But does this biblical law of tithing apply to Christians? In responding to this question, we believe it is essential to consider two separate questions. Are Christians *required* to tithe? And *should* Christians tithe? We believe the answer to the first question is "no." In his substantial work *Jesus and Money*, respected New Testament scholar Ben Witherington III reminds us that Christians no longer live under the strictures of Levitical law where tithing requirements are interwoven with requirements such as stoning disobedient children, avoiding tattoos, and other laws Christians have never felt bound to observe.[12] Witherington concludes that the law of tithing is no more binding on Christians than any other aspects of Mosaic law.

The Christian motivation to give is not grounded in the law but in a voluntary response to God's love and generosity. Jesus addressed the subject of tithing only once. In his series of "woe to you" denunciations of the Pharisees, he says, "Woe to you, scribes and Pharisees, hypocrites. For you tithe mint, dill, and cumin, and have neglected the weightier matters of the law: Justice and mercy and faith. It is these you ought to have practiced without neglecting the others" (Matthew 23:23). Jesus doesn't condemn the practice of tithing in this passage. He clearly indicates that the practice of tithing must be viewed within the larger context of faithful living.

Some who have been taught that tithing is a biblical command and the immutable law of God are surprised to learn that the emphasis on tithing in American Protestantism didn't emerge until the late nineteenth and early twentieth centuries when older methods for financing the church, such as state support and pew rentals, gave way.[13] Indeed, the whole paradigm of voluntary giving and stewardship is a relatively recent development. Through most of European history, for example, the nobility supported the church, keeping up church buildings on their lands and paying the local priest.

But to say that tithing is not required of Christians does not mean the amount of one's giving is an inconsequential matter. Jesus told a rich young ruler to sell everything he had and give the money to the poor (Matthew 19:21; Mark 10:21). He declared that salvation had come when Zacchaeus pledged half his possessions to the poor (Luke 19:8–9). He commended the widow at the temple for contributing her two small copper coins (Mark 12:42–43). In none of these cases was the percentage a tithe. And yet these levels of giving were acceptable to Jesus because they represented a significant sacrifice undertaken genuinely as an expression of faith. For Christians, the ultimate measure of giving is sacrifice. There is nothing magical about 10 percent or any other percentage. But it is notable that in each of these examples the percentage far exceeded a tithe. Saying Christians aren't *required* to tithe doesn't let us off the hook.

The biblical concept of tithing is abused in contemporary practice by anyone who maintains that it is a requirement, the only acceptable standard of giving, or that God's blessings are contingent on tithing. Paradoxically, overemphasizing tithing can put a ceiling on the gifts of those for whom a sacrificial level of giving would be more than 10 percent. And it creates the misimpression that giving 10 percent to God means one can do as one pleases with the remaining 90 percent. Interpreted correctly, tithing should reinforce the belief that everything, not just 10 percent, belongs to God and must be stewarded for God's purposes.

On balance, however, there is much to commend in the practice of tithing. It is deeply rooted in Scripture. A commitment to tithing enacts the biblical principles of giving purposefully, proportionately, and from first fruits. Since the average percentage given by churchgoers today is far less than ten percent, tithing is an appropriately challenging standard that would help the vast majority of Christians achieve more meaningful levels of generosity. With these things in mind, *should* Christians tithe? We believe it is commendable for people to tithe or seek to grow toward tithing, while we acknowledge that a sacrificial gift can constitute any percentage and that some people need to be giving more than 10 percent. Throughout this book, we lift up tithing as an important goal in Christian giving.

Almost inevitably, two questions arise related to tithing. Should a tithe be calculated on your pretax income or take-home pay? And can one's tithe include giving to charities other than the church? These questions rarely come from those tithing their net income wondering whether they should give based on their gross, or from those whose tithe includes other charities considering whether they should give more to their church. Like the questions the

Pharisees posed to test Jesus, these questions are often inauthentic, intended to discredit tithing by reducing it to a legalism. While credible Christian leaders make good arguments on both sides of these questions, we believe the gracious response is to say "Amen!" to everyone tithing their net income or giving 10 percent to church and other charities. Their generous hearts are likely to lead them to even greater generosity.

LEARNING AND LEADING ALONG THE WAY

When we ask groups of seminary students how they might share these beliefs about faith and giving, their initial response is almost always to plan a Bible study or a sermon series. The problem is that, if you announce a sermon series on "What the Bible Teaches about Giving," a good percentage of your congregation will stay home that Sunday or tune it out, because they assume it's a funding pitch. Same thing with a small group study. The people likely to show up are those who least need to hear the message.

Preaching and teaching on stewardship themes is far more effective when it happens along the way, not just on Stewardship Sunday or during a commitment campaign. Congregations that succeed in nurturing a culture of generosity find ways to weave these beliefs into their ongoing preaching and teaching. This more subtle but persistent approach also signals that faithfulness in giving is part and parcel of the Christian life, not something that stands alone. Fortunately, there are excellent resources available on integrating stewardship themes across the lectionary cycle and liturgical year.

Chapter 4

Pledging and Commitment Campaigns

Making pledges is one method of instituting thoughtful, deliberate, regular giving. Smith and Emerson found that in every denomination studied those who filled out pledge cards contributed significantly more money than those who did not.[1] They report that "pledging Lutherans gave 45 percent more money than non-pledging Lutherans, pledging Catholics gave 77 percent more than non-pledging Catholics, and pledging Baptists gave 34 percent more money than non-pledging Baptists."[2] The researchers acknowledge some of these pledgers may have been predisposed to give more even in the absence of a pledge. But they conclude on the basis of excellent theoretical reasons and observed empirical data that "engaging in the process of annual planning, deciding, and pledging as a structured means of regular, deliberate, and consistent financial giving itself influences giving to higher levels."[3] Overall, they concluded that the degree of planning involved in giving decisions significantly influences how much is given both in terms of dollars and the percentage of income given.[4]

More recent research on the economic practices of congregations by the Lake Institute on Faith and Giving found that 70 percent of the mainline Protestant congregations conduct an annual pledge drive and stewardship campaign.[5] But looking across different traditions, pledging is not the norm. Only 45 percent of congregations in the Lake Institute study conduct an annual stewardship campaign; among those, only 64 percent explicitly ask for a pledge of a certain amount.[6] And overall, they found similar increases in revenue among congregations with annual stewardship campaigns and those without them.[7] This suggests that while a pledge is effective in helping people be more deliberate and regular in giving, it is not the only method. Churches can also encourage consistent, regular giving via regular appeals in worship, providing weekly offering envelopes, sending regular giving statements, and encouraging recurring online donations or automatic bank transfers.

But a pledge drive or stewardship campaign isn't just about enhancing giving totals. It is a time for spiritual reflection and mission education and a punctuation point that gives emphasis to ongoing efforts to nurture generosity. A good campaign is a harvest that gathers the fruits of generosity cultivated throughout the year. If you don't sow the seeds or tend the growth, the harvest won't be abundant. But conversely, if you sow and water but fail to reap, the full abundance of the harvest is not realized. While a commitment campaign doesn't substitute for other aspects of ongoing, year-round stewardship ministry, a well-executed campaign can be the combine machine that brings home the harvest of generosity.

Before going further, it's helpful to consider terminology. First, what is a pledge? The very notion of a pledge troubles some people. In certain branches of the Christian family, pledges are seen as akin to swearing oaths. Some older adults, particularly those with memories shaped by the Great Depression, are afraid of making pledges because they fear being unable to fulfill them. For these reasons, some churches prefer the term "estimate of giving." It's important to communicate that neither a pledge nor a giving estimate is a legally binding contract. They can be modified if someone's circumstances change. A pledge is a promise between the giver and God shared with the church for the purpose of being more faithful, accountable, and generous.

Second, terms like pledge appeal, annual campaign, commitment campaign, stewardship drive, and similar variants can have slightly different meanings in different contexts. But for the purposes of this discussion, the terms are used interchangeably to refer to an orchestrated effort involving a concentrated period of communication, preaching, and teaching to encourage church participants to offer commitments in the form of pledges or giving estimates.

PRACTICAL STRATEGIES FOR EFFECTIVE COMMITMENT CAMPAIGNS

Emphasize the Mission Not the Budget

In many churches the pledge appeal is closely tied to the annual budget. The goal is to raise the revenue needed to fund the budget. A line item budget is often attached to the appeal letter. But trying to meet a line item budget isn't a very effective way to motivate people to give. Sure, a few people want to study every bit of it. And, for the sake of financial transparency, everyone should know the budget is available if they request it. But most people don't give to support budgets or balance sheets. They give to support people and programs.

So, build your message around mission, vision, and purpose. Tell stories. Talk about hopes. Share results and success stories. And never base the appeal on the church's need for money, no matter how badly it is needed. People are reluctant to invest in an institution that signals that it is circling the drain. They want to support strong, vibrant organizations and compelling causes.

How can you avoid a campaign focused on raising the budget? Some churches wait to formulate their budget until the results of the campaign are known. Another strategy is preparing a narrative or ministry-impact budget that converts your line item budget into an inspiring, visually attractive document that relates all expenditures to ministry goals rather than accounting categories. A narrative budget demonstrates how money is filtered through the church to touch lives and accomplish ministry objectives.

Tailor Your Approach to Different Types of Givers

Many churches have a one-size-fits-all approach to their annual stewardship appeal. Everyone in the congregation receives the same "Dear Friend" letter inviting them to offer up their tithe for the coming year. While this approach is simple and easy to execute, it ignores the reality that every church has people at various points in their journey of generosity. And approaching them all with the same appeal just doesn't make sense from a spiritual or a developmental perspective. It is more effective to tailor different messages to different categories of givers—your most generous givers, good givers with room to grow, those who contribute but do not pledge, those who do not regularly contribute, and new members, for example. Yes, this means that someone needs to be paying attention to who's who, where they are spiritually, and what they give. But the need to communicate with people about their giving in meaningful and appropriate ways is one of the best arguments in favor of allowing responsible people proper access to giving records.

Acknowledge Those Who Cannot Give

At any given time, some people in your congregation will be experiencing financial challenges—the loss of a job, a broken marriage, a death, or illness in the family. It's important to signal that these people are still valued members of the community. For example, "If you are out of work or have had a financial setback, tell us on your commitment card that you cannot make a pledge at this time. This is our time to help you. Above all, don't ever fail to attend just because you can't contribute." Such a message speaks not just to those currently in financial distress. It lets everyone else know they belong to a church that is sensitive to people's financial reality. And this will make them feel more comfortable about committing.

Get Personal

Why do people give money to support churches and other causes? The number one reason is because they were asked. And people are more likely to give based on their relationship with the person asking than on the merits of the cause. There's nothing better in any kind of fundraising than a personal invitation, so strive to communicate in the most personal way possible. A personalized letter is better than a form letter. A handwritten note better than a letter. A phone call better than a note. A one-on-one visit is best of all, which is why visitation is a key element in building campaigns or major fund drives.

Many churches have moved away from canvasing every member for pledges because the task seems so overwhelming. But just because you can't visit *everybody* doesn't mean you shouldn't visit *anybody*. You might develop a plan to visit some fraction of the congregation each year with the goal of visiting everyone over the course of several years. Or you might ask, "What visits are most critical or impactful?" Newer members or those who have increased their level of engagement might be on your priority list. But don't overlook your most generous givers because those already significantly invested in your ministry are most likely to continue to increase their giving.

Handwritten notes or letters can also personalize your pledge appeals. One approach is a personal letter writing campaign led by a team of commitment leaders, each assigned to write to a group of ten to twenty fellow church members. To the extent possible, these assignments should be based on relational ties or shared affinities so that the leaders can write heartfelt, personal appeals. Group gatherings can also add a face-to-face dimension to your campaign. Existing groups, such as Sunday school classes or small groups, can reinforce your campaign message. Or you can plan special meetings or house parties. Storytelling and personal witness are very personal, effective ways to communicate. So, invite discussion around questions such as "What difference has the church made in your life or in the lives of others?" or "Why do you give." Invite people to dream about the future of the church and share their hopes.

Communicate. Communicate. Communicate.

A commitment campaign is essentially a communication exercise. You'll want to develop a comprehensive communication strategy that takes advantage of all available means of communication. Start with a theme that will catch people's attention, capture the ethos of your church, and tie together preaching, teaching, and testimony. Consider what printed materials you need—perhaps a brochure, special stationery, or thank you cards in addition to your pledge card. How might you use email, social media, and online giving or pledging? A brief video or slide show is an effective way to illustrate your mission and remind people of all that goes on at your church. And don't forget the church newsletter, the pastor's weekly email, the website, visual displays, and banners.

Follow Up

No matter how inspiring and thorough your plan, some sizable percentage of your congregation isn't going to respond to the initial pledge appeal. To finish strong, you need a strategy to bring into the fold those who require a bit more encouragement. Decide in advance how you will reach out to late responders through notes, phone calls, or follow-up visits. But even if you need to contact people repeatedly, avoid shaming or treating them like deadbeats. A positive, invitational appeal is always more effective than one based on guilt or institutional need. Be sure to reserve some time and energy for follow up, acknowledgment, and continuing communication that can bring new people into the circle of giving and lay the groundwork for enhanced generosity.

Say Thank You

Congregations that want to inspire giving thank their givers. And one important juncture for saying thank you is when donors make their pledges. It's easy to overlook this critical step, unless you have a plan in place at the start of your campaign. One simple approach is to preprint notecards with a brief generic thank you message. Then ask your pastor or campaign chair to add a very brief handwritten note. If you preaddress envelopes for everyone solicited for a pledge, it's easier to get these notes in the mail promptly. If you're sending more formal acknowledgment letters, draft in advance three variants—one for those who are continuing their pledges at the same level, one for those who have increased their pledges, and one for those pledging for the first time.

Give It Time

These steps require planning and coordination. Start early and plan ahead. Construct a realistic timeline for your campaign that allows enough time on the front end for planning and preparation and enough on the back end for follow up and acknowledgments. A good timeline can also connect campaign activities with the liturgical calendar, preaching topics, and other major church activities. A good timeline will keep your work on track.

Keep It Fresh

Have you ever found that when you try a new approach to something you usually get a better response? Whether you're soliciting pledges, recruiting volunteers, or inviting people into membership, trying something new usually engenders a positive response, at least for a while. The response to any approach may start to wane over time. Remember that there is usually no one best way of asking people to give or serve. Some people respond better to one approach and others to something different. Each new approach you try will resonate with a different group of people.

If your congregation has conducted a fall commitment campaign in the same way for as long as anyone can remember, trying something different will generally yield positive results. If you do a letter writing campaign one year, you might consider a campaign built around house parties the next year, for example. If you need ideas, there are many good published resources available with everything necessary to implement campaigns built around different modalities and themes.

Build a Team

The most effective commitment campaigns are led by a broad-based team of lay leaders. The pastor's involvement and support are very critical. But taking the pastor out of the lead role minimizes the perception that they are appealing out of self-interest. This fear of being perceived as "asking for money for themselves" is one of the main reasons so many pastors feel awkward talking about money.[8] Let other leaders spearhead the actual appeal and ask the pastor to focus on preaching, teaching, and vision casting.

A team approach builds investment in the process and creates a sense of ownership in the outcome. If your team is broadly representative of the congregation, it creates natural connections with people of different ages and different areas of ministry. And getting lay leaders involved is a great way to educate them about stewardship. Who might be part of such a team? It's generally not the green-eyeshade accountant types that are found on church finance committees. You might be lucky enough to have people in your congregation who have led giving campaigns for other organizations. But at the end of the day, your most effective stewardship leaders will be those people who are deeply in love with the Lord and with your church.

GETTING STARTED

If these ideas and strategies seem overwhelming, focus on just one during your next commitment cycle. And if your congregation is small, take heart!

Things that can require a great deal of planning and organizing in a large congregation often come naturally in a smaller church. For example, an every-member canvas or a personal letter writing campaign is far easier to execute in a smaller church.

What if your church has never done a pledge campaign before but wants to start? As with any major change, it can be helpful to start small. You're unlikely to get everyone to adopt a new practice by simply declaring, "This year, we expect everyone to pledge." In fact, such a declaration could engender opposition and backlash. An incremental strategy would be to quietly approach your most reliable, regular givers first. Ask them to pledge what they would normally give as a way to get the ball rolling. And then gradually extend the appeal to others until you have a critical mass. At that point, you can introduce pledging to the congregation as a practice that many in the church have already adopted as a way of being more faithful and deliberate in their giving.

THINKING BEYOND THE PLEDGE AND
THE OFFERING PLATE

Having established that pledging can help people be more intentional and generous givers and having shown how a pledge campaign can be an important component in an overall stewardship strategy, we now want to interject a word of caution. Many churches, especially mainline churches, conduct a pledge campaign each fall like clockwork, but then they forget about generosity and giving until pledge season rolls around again the next year. Or they put so much emphasis on pledging that they end up ignoring people who aren't ready or willing to pledge.

In these liminal times, many established patterns of congregational life are no longer adequate to the challenges of the day. We believe that making offerings to God is an essential act of Christian worship, but we live in a day when even our most stalwart church members attend worship more sporadically. We know that pledging helps people be more intentional and generous givers, but a generation skeptical of institutional allegiances is not nearly as quick as their forebears to take membership vows or sign pledge cards. We are called to shape people for lives of generosity, but we wonder if our institutions can remain healthy enough to fulfill this critical calling.

In a post-Christian, post-attractional era, standard approaches to stewardship and generosity are stressed and strained, as are our paradigms of worship, evangelism, membership, and faith formation. The challenges of our day demand creative "both/and" thinking. We must reaffirm the basics of faith and generosity foundational to our theology, identity, and practice. At the same time, we must embrace new practices, including a more developmental approach to fostering generosity and moving boldly into the realm of digital giving and fundraising. In the next two chapters, we explore the need to think beyond the pledge and the offering plate as we seek to introduce a new generation to the joys of generosity.

Chapter 5

Fostering Faithful Giving

Many congregations simply take it for granted that people come into their churches knowing the basics of faith and giving. Or they assume people will learn by osmosis sitting in the pew week after week, participating in the offering, becoming more regular and more generous until they eventually become pledgers, tithers, or sacrificial givers. This assumed pipeline has sprung some major leaks. Congregations need to be more proactive and creative in helping people move from first-time givers to sacrificial generosity.

A developmental approach to stewardship ministry borrows some of the best techniques of secular fundraising to enhance generosity in the church. A developmental perspective acknowledges that different individuals have different giving histories, motivations, and levels of spiritual maturity. Accordingly, appeals based on where people are, spiritually and developmentally, are more effective than a one-size-fits-all blanket approach. The recommendation in the previous chapter of crafting different campaign messages for different categories of givers is an example of a developmentally sensitive approach. It's more than just good fundraising. It's a way to help people take their next faithful step as stewards and disciples.

KNOW YOUR GIVERS

A first key step is to analyze giving patterns in your congregation. Drawing on contribution records, sort your donors from highest to lowest. Remember, the purpose isn't to judge. It's to understand where people are spiritually and developmentally. Typically, in churches and other charities, there is a relatively small number of contributors giving at the highest levels and many more people contributing in the lower giving ranges. This pattern is called a giving pyramid. The small number of large donors is at the apex of the pyramid and the large number of smaller donors forms the base of the pyramid. A giving pyramid analysis reveals that the small percentage of larger donors at the top accounts for a very significant percentage of the dollars given to a church while the much larger number of small donors at the bottom of the pyramid accounts for a relatively small percentage of dollars given.

Smith and Emerson's research confirmed this same pattern of giving when they looked across the board at what all American Christians give. They found that the top 5 percent of most generous givers accounts for almost 60 percent of all the dollars contributed, that the vast majority give very little, and that one in five American Christians gives literally nothing to church or other charities.[1] You may find this shocking, but it's highly likely that an analysis of giving levels in your congregation would reveal a similar pattern.

Armed with a realistic understanding of what's actually going on, you can ask some key questions. How can your church help the people who aren't giving at all get started? How can you help more modest givers grow in generosity? And how can you continue to motivate and inspire the most generous givers on whom your ministry depends financially?

PRACTICAL STRATEGIES TO INSPIRE
GENEROUS GIVING

Developmental stewardship also acknowledges that good fundraising plays a role in good stewardship ministry. Some church leaders dismiss fundraising as distasteful, irreligious, or gimmicky. However, effective giving appeals can be just what's needed to help potential givers begin their journey of generosity. Churches must guard against an overreliance on fundraising at the expense of helping people develop a more mature understanding of Christian generosity. Effective fundraising techniques can never lead everyone in a church to give up to their potential. But savvy giving appeals can function as on-ramps for new givers, educating them about the church's mission, and helping them experience the joy of giving.

Address Nongivers Separately

You may be surprised to learn that within every congregation there is a substantial cohort of people who do not contribute at all. Congregations that study their giving patterns typically discover that upwards of 20 to 30 percent of members and participants are noncontributors. Some may be new to the church. Some are younger. Some may be less active than they once were. Some are your Easter and Christmas crowd. Some may not understand how giving in the church works. Some think it doesn't apply to them for any number of reasons. And some just have never gotten with the program. It's tempting for insiders to assume these people are deadbeats and freeloaders. But that's the wrong attitude. Assume God has placed these people in your church for a reason and they just need a little extra encouragement.

People give before they pledge or tithe. That bears repeating. People give before they pledge or tithe. If you constantly stress pledging and tithing when addressing matters of giving, these folks are likely to disregard the message. After all, why would someone who's not giving a dime to the church pay attention when you ask them to give 10 percent? It's not that pledging and tithing are unimportant. It's just not the right place to start the conversation for this segment of people. Remember, we must first teach people *why* they should give before they are ready to consider *how* to give and *how much* to give.

When your church conducts a stewardship campaign, ask noncontributors simply to make a gift instead of sending them a pledge card. Remind them of the good work that the church does and how they can be a part of it. Easter, Christmas, and the end of the year are other logical times to ask them to give. Don't expect a huge rate of return. Communicating regularly with nongivers in a positive, inviting manner can build their sense of connection. If some of your more active members or leaders are noncontributors, some gentle, pastoral conversation may be in order to discover what keeps them from giving and how they might get started.

Provide Special Giving Opportunities

Newer givers are often motivated by specific, tangible needs. They understand the importance of contributing $50 if it is needed to fuel the church van for the youth mission outing or $100 to purchase groceries for the food pantry. Such special giving opportunities tell a story. They educate potential givers about the church's mission, and they allow a new giver to experience the joy of contributing to something worthwhile. Church finance experts have long debated whether this kind of designated giving is appropriate. "The church shouldn't nickel-and-dime people," they argue. "Isn't it more important to encourage people to make a sacrificial, ongoing commitment?" Or, "Special appeals will never pay the utility bills!" Probably they won't. But newer givers are rarely motivated to give out of institutional loyalty. The trick is to use special appeals strategically to educate and motivate new givers, while at the same time encouraging them toward regular, ongoing gifts. For example, if someone contributes five jars of peanut butter for the food pantry, you might next ask them to give $50 to support the project and later ask them to make a gift to the church, explaining how the food pantry is part of the church's ongoing mission.

Build Involvement

If someone asked you to guess the top ten givers in your church, whose names would be on your list? You might imagine that the person driving the fanciest car or owning that beautiful second home in a nearby vacation community would be among the top givers. But you'd probably be wrong unless that individual was also deeply involved in the mission of the church. The strongest predictor of how much someone gives to their church is their level of activity and engagement, not their level of income. Business leaders and fundraisers know that people support what they help to create. Active engagement builds agency, investment in outcomes, and a sense of shared ownership. So, the best way to get people interested in giving is to get them actively involved. Invite that person who gave five jars of peanut butter to join the feeding ministry team, and he or she will start connecting the dots between giving to the church and this important work.

Ask Mature Givers to Encourage New Givers

Many charities use matching gift challenges to incentivize giving. This approach may seem gimmicky or risky in its acknowledgment that not everyone gives at the same level. But what if we embraced the idea that more mature givers could encourage newer givers? One Texas church adopted the "secular" idea of matching gifts to draw the congregation together for the purpose of encouraging generosity. New givers were invited to make a giving commitment for the first time, and mature Christians were invited to encourage them by providing a match above their normal pledge. "Of dozens who were asked, not a single person declined," reported the pastor. "In fact, several matching donors gave more than requested and others approached us to ask if they could join the matching group." The result was a 23 percent increase in commitments, which included many first time commitments.[2] Spiritual mentorship is a time-tested, biblically sound approach to faith formation. Why shouldn't it also be a way of developing disciples through giving?

Ask for Specific Amounts

As a general rule in fundraising, it's more effective to approach a donor with a request for a specific amount. Unless you suggest how much to give, givers will not have a point of reference for judging what kind of response is needed or appropriate and they will probably just continue to do what they have always done. To encourage modest or mid-level donors to grow in their giving, ask them for a specific dollar amount or a specific percentage increase. For example, you might say, "We are grateful for your support of $1,000 last year. We hope this year you will increase your annual gift to $1,250." One Lutheran church used this approach and the result was a 30 percent increase in support for their annual budget.[3] Everyone is familiar with charitable donation requests that include a response card with check-off boxes. "Yes! Count me in! I will contribute: ρ $1,000, ρ $500, ρ $250, ρ $100, or ρ $___." This type of response mechanism is quite effective when raising funds for mission trips, missionary support, special projects, small-scale capital projects, or other targeted, well-defined needs. Without this guidance you might get a lot of $15 or $25 gifts simply because you haven't let people know the level of gifts needed to reach your goal.

Solicit Major Gifts

What about those who have given the same respectable amount to the church every year for decades, but are not giving up to their potential? They likely tune out messages about growing in giving because they believe they're already doing their part. Lots of people never increase their giving because they're never asked or given a compelling reason to do so. And most congregations never think of approaching someone with a specific personal ask outside of the context of a capital or building campaign. But as pledging and weekly offerings wane, some congregations are looking to the example of other nonprofits and soliciting specific gifts, large and small, to fund ongoing ministry. This is best done personally in a face-to-face meeting with a request that connects to the donor's interests or concerns. For example, a longtime Sunday school teacher could be invited to make a special gift to support an increase in the children's ministry budget. Creating a wish list of needs or projects can jumpstart this type of special giving. For example, the burgeoning feeding ministry with such enthusiastic new leadership needs $35,000 for a van, $6,000 for a freezer, and $1,000 to purchase supplies.

Don't Ignore the Most Generous Givers

What about the faithful few who have already given so much? You might assume it isn't fair to ask them to do even more. However, as counterintuitive as it may seem, the people most likely to continue to increase their giving are those already giving at a high level. They have proven themselves dedicated to your mission and faithful in their giving practices. While it's important to encourage newer givers, it's equally important to acknowledge that your ministry depends on the continued generosity of major givers and to treat them accordingly. Stay as connected as possible with these individuals. Regularly express gratitude and let them know the importance of their leadership in giving.

GROWING IN GENEROSITY—GROWING IN DISCIPLESHIP

How do such appeals relate to our spiritual imperative to give? Some may see them as antithetical to encouraging giving for spiritual reasons. On the contrary, helping people give more generously is a spiritual imperative. Generous behavior is closely linked to spiritual growth. Things that help people grow spiritually—Bible study, regular worship attendance, participation in prayer circles and small groups, and so on—are closely correlated with growth in giving. Not surprisingly, the opposite is also true. Becoming more generous helps people grow in faith and discipleship as well. When we invest in the mission of God, our hearts follow. Inviting people to experience the joy of generosity provides a starting point for understanding the spiritual significance of giving. Our work to foster generous giving always occurs within the larger context of our biblical and theological beliefs. For that reason, fundraising must always be done with integrity and for the best reasons. When it is, it advances God's mission of generosity, reinforces our theology of giving, and helps people grow in faith and generosity.

Chapter 6

The Digital Offering Plate

Digital and online giving are vital to healthy congregational stewardship in the twenty-first century. Most people today, even older adults, use credit and debit cards, online banking services, direct deposits, automatic bill payment, and apps to conduct routine financial transactions. And this is especially true of younger generations who have never done it any other way. They don't even have checkbooks and rarely carry cash. Yet most congregations have not kept pace with this reality.

In many churches, the list of ways people can give is quite short. You can give during the offering if you attend worship. You can mail a check to the church office. Or you can bring your gift to the church office. Think of what all three of these options have in common. They all rely on cash or checks! Yet the use of checks has declined dramatically in recent years. The Federal Reserve reported that from 2000 to 2015, the number of checks written by consumers fell from 19.3 billion to 7.1 billion. A recent survey by the Federal Reserve found that 39 percent of adults had not written a check during the previous year.[1] The Federal Reserve found that writing checks was the preferred method of payment for only 3 percent of people. For many people today, their check to the church is the only check they write all week.[2]

The Lake Institute's 2019 report on congregational economic practices found that only about half of congregations studied had a digital giving option. Not surprisingly, larger congregations are more likely to have online giving options, while smaller churches tend to rely more on traditional means of receiving gifts. Overall, the vast majority of congregations still receive the bulk of their contributions through the offering plate with checks still accounting for four times the average amount received digitally or in cash.[3]

ADVANTAGES OF ONLINE GIVING

What are some of the advantages of expanding electronic giving? First, it is more convenient for the large and growing segment of worshippers who pay almost all their regular bills and payments through online or automated systems and desire to make their church gift in the same manner. There's a reason why movie theaters don't limit your choice to one or two movies per week and why utilities don't require all customers to come to their offices to pay their monthly bills. People today expect and appreciate convenience and choice.

Digital giving also helps a church sustain a steady and predictable income stream. Receiving donations online maintains cash flow and softens slumps when vacations or bad weather keep people from attending church, especially when donors set up recurring weekly or monthly donations. Churches without electronic giving capacities learned this lesson the hard way in the spring of 2020 when coronavirus prevention measures prevented worship gatherings all around the globe.

Perhaps most importantly, there is mounting evidence that online giving results in higher levels of generosity. The Lake Institute found a positive relationship between congregations that embrace innovative donation technologies and reported growth in revenue.[4] Data from the 2015 Faith Communities Today survey indicated that having online collection methods increased per capita giving by $114, while emphasizing electronic giving quite a bit or a lot raised it by $300 per person.[5] And the relationship between online donations and enhanced generosity will likely increase as the digital economy grows even more dominant and as congregations become more open to receiving and appealing for electronic gifts.

EXPANDING GIVING OPTIONS

How much of your church's giving comes in checks or cash? If 90 percent or more of your giving comes through these means, you may want to assess other giving options. The goal isn't simply to keep up with the times but to remove unnecessary barriers for those who want to contribute to your mission. It's not about technology but rather mission enhancement. Fortunately, a range of options is available to facilitate electronic giving, some of which do not require investments in major technology upgrades.

Online Bill Pay Banking

Most banks offer online bill payment systems through their websites. Online bill payment is a secure electronic service that allows customers to pay bills without having to write checks and mail them. Online bill payment usually is tied to a checking account from which funds are withdrawn electronically for payment of onetime or recurring bills. Many banks offer this service to their customers free of charge. And no setup is required from the church.

Automatic Bank Withdrawal

This method of electronic funds transfer permits members to set up an automatic recurring contribution, usually set for once or twice a month. The transfer of funds (sometimes referred to as direct payments or ACH payments) occurs through the Automated Clearing House, a U.S. financial network used to transfer money from one back account to another without using checks, credit cards, wire transfers, or cash. Many churches have used this for years. Your bank can advise you on what's required to set up a regular transfer by direct deposit.

Online Giving through the Church Website

As more and more people engage in internet commerce, churches are increasingly using their websites to receive online contributions. There are several third-party vendors that specialize in helping churches set up and maintain online giving portals where congregants can create accounts, log in, and manage their donations. Once this system is in place, access through smartphone apps, text to give options, and mobile card readers can also be added.

Mobile Card Readers

"Square" is an example of a small device that plugs into a smartphone or tablet to create an electronic pay station accepting payments from major credit or debit cards and from cellphone virtual wallets. A good Internet connection is required, and someone must be available to operate the pay station. Some congregations use mobile card readers in their sanctuaries to receive offerings. Card readers are also useful at fundraisers and special events where payments or fees are collected.

Giving Kiosks

One of the edgiest innovations is the installation of one or more giving kiosks in a church for credit or debit card giving. They look like ATM machines and they can be purchased or leased. These kiosks are typically placed in a church's narthex or in the worship space so that congregants can make their offering during worship, or as they come and go.

PRACTICAL STRATEGIES FOR IMPLEMENTING DIGITAL GIVING

Although electronic transactions are ubiquitous in other facets of life, evidence suggests that digital giving is underused even in churches that make it available. There is clearly work to be done to help church folks see it as an appropriate way of making an offering to God. Keep in mind that you are providing options for those who wish to use them. But don't underestimate how quickly people can change their habits. When churches began using offering envelopes, for example, the practice seemed strange at first but quickly caught on. In 1990, most Americans regarded paying for groceries by credit card as peculiar. Now cards cover about 65 percent of food sales.

Do Your Homework

Before proposing any changes, research your options carefully. Richard Rogers's *E-Giving Guide for Every Congregation*[6] is a fine primer on the subject. And a great deal of information is readily available online. Look also to the example of other churches in your community or your denomination with effective online giving systems, especially those like your church in size and character. Your denomination or judicatory can be another source of advice. And some have special partnerships or discounts with preferred online service vendors.

As you consider options, it's important to answer some questions first. What types of electronic transactions are already familiar to your members? How will electronic transactions interface with your banking, bookkeeping, or data management systems? What are the fees and costs? Who needs to be involved in the day-to-day management? And what kind of setup, training, or testing is required to get the system up and running? Make sure to solicit input from as many people as possible and include all finance leaders, staff, and the appropriate governing groups in these conversations.

Address Concerns about Credit Card Debt and Transaction Fees

It's important to address openly two lingering concerns that keep many churches from entering the realm of electronic giving. The first is fear that accepting credit cards might add to the burden of those carrying high levels of consumer debt. But there's little evidence suggesting that charitable giving is the cause of accelerating credit card balances. The purpose of receiving gifts through credit cards is never to encourage people to give beyond their means but simply to provide a more convenient way to give. A more immediate way to help church members avoid excessive debt is for churches to offer instruction or counseling on managing personal finances, a subject addressed in the next part of this book.

Another common concern relates to the fees or costs associated with certain types of electronic giving. While the impact of fees certainly should be explored, it's important to communicate that these costs are far outweighed by the positive benefits of expanding the array of giving options, as is the case with electronic transactions in any other sector of the economy. Electronic giving also reduces the time and resources devoted to processing and depositing checks as well as the risks of dealing with cash. Moreover, e-giving platforms intended for church use are designed to integrate with commonly used data management systems, streamlining bookkeeping and accounting functions.

Launch New Giving Options Strategically.

A Florida church wanted to create an opportunity for every member to become familiar with a new online giving feature on its website. So, they unveiled the new feature with a challenge to the congregation. As a way of testing the new system, they challenged everyone to go to the website and make a small donation for the upcoming Vacation Bible School. Not only did they received gifts from congregants that day, but they also received a $500 gift from someone who just happened to be visiting, demonstrating to everyone the potential of this method of receiving gifts.[7]

Keep Information about Online Giving Front and Center

Some churches undertake the work of setting up online contribution systems but do little to promote their availability. They assume an initial announcement or two is sufficient to get the word out. Then they go back to business as usual, leaving those interested in electronic giving options to seek them out on their own. Most churches that do not see good results in introducing electronic giving fail to share enough information in a consistent and generous way.

What are some ways to keep electronic giving options in front of your congregants and other donors? Make sure anyone landing on your church website can easily find their way to the donation page. Your website should also include information on any other available online giving options. Information on electronic giving should be a standing element of your worship bulletins. If you livestream worship, an invitation to give online should appear on the webpage where people access the livestream. Your weekly invitation to offering should always include a brief reminder of how attendees can participate digitally. If your church receives pledges, make sure all pledgers receive information on how to fulfill their commitment by setting up a recurring online gift. And similar information should be included when contribution statements or reminders are mailed to donors.

Celebrate Online Giving in Worship

Many people don't give online because the ritual of participating in the offering is a deeply engrained habit. While making an offering is an essential element of worship, it doesn't matter whether that offering comes in the form of nickels and dimes, paper bills or checks, automatic withdrawals, or online contributions. It is all acceptable to God. Remember that an offering is a meaningful form of worship because it represents a tangible sacrifice of something important to us. When or how it is delivered does not matter. That said, it's important that your offering rituals acknowledge that online gifts are an acceptable way to participate. In addition to mentioning online donations in the invitation to give, make sure when dedicating the offering to mention that gifts received electronically, by mail, and so forth are also being blessed.

Many churches create laminated cards saying something to the effect of "I have made my gift online" and place them in pew racks where the offering envelopes are kept. Online givers can place these cards in the offering plates or baskets to symbolize their participation in the offering. And these cards do double duty if they also have information explaining how people can give electronically.

THE PROMISE OF DIGITAL GIVING

Electronic giving is more than just a convenience for church attenders who would otherwise give on Sunday mornings and a way for churches to receive income more predictably. Electronic giving is an essential way of enhancing generosity and connecting with new givers. In the dominant paradigm of church giving, we wait until someone comes through the door of our church to invite them to give. And we only ask them to give when they attend on Sunday. But in an era when fewer and fewer people find their way into churches and even our regulars attend only a couple of Sundays a month, churches that don't expand their generosity efforts are fishing in a smaller and smaller pond.

Electronic giving has the potential to reach younger generations, occasional attenders, and even people who don't yet attend church by leapfrogging beyond our traditional reliance on the pledge and the offering plate. As the church of the future increasingly moves online, so too will the church's ministry of generosity. This future requires not only the capacity to *receive* digital gifts but also the skill in *soliciting* gifts from people beyond the reach of Sunday services. In the Internet age, virtually all other nonprofits cultivate their donor base through electronic communication and electronic giving. And forward-thinking churches are taking a page from their playbook.

When inviting people to support your mission, imagine the potential if, instead of just preaching to the choir, you sent an attractive email with an online giving link to everyone who's part of your church's wider circle of influence, including those who attend less frequently, shut-ins, retirees living in different parts of the county, past visitors, occasional contributors, friends and neighbors, community partners. All these people likely care about what your church does, even if they aren't always there on Sunday. Imagine if some of these members and friends shared your appeal on social media because they are inspired by the work of the food pantry or Vacation Bible School or the upcoming mission trip. Then imagine that the people reached through social media were also interested in getting involved. This is how the church of the twenty-first century will fund ministry, attract new people to its mission, and help them participate in the generosity of God—but only if we are bold and creative in embracing the potential of online giving and online connections.

Part II

STEWARDSHIP

Chapter 7

The Biblical Concept of Stewardship

A biblical understanding of stewardship begins with the simple affirmation that *everything* belongs to God. As the Psalmist so eloquently wrote, "The earth is the Lord's and all that is in it, the world, and those who live in it; for God has founded it on the seas, and established it on the rivers" (Psalm 24:1–2). To understand that everything belongs to God means we don't own anything, not even ourselves. Whatever we have or control comes to us through the grace of God. We are to hold it in trust and use it for God's purpose and glory. We are not owners but rather stewards of the things God has entrusted to us. This doctrine of stewardship is the second core theological affirmation that shapes a Christian understanding of money and possessions. It rests on the foundation of the doctrine of the generosity of God. God entrusts things to our care by virtue of God's generosity. And by being wise stewards of the things God entrusts to us, we can participate in God's generosity and help bring forth God's abundance.

At one level, it may seem obvious to declare that everything belongs to God. But at another level, it is a profoundly countercultural belief. Private property and private ownership are bedrock principles of American capitalism. At some level, we all operate with the assumption that we are entitled to *True* what we earn and what we have. And so, the church's task in teaching biblical stewardship is quite challenging.

WHAT IS A STEWARD?

In the ancient world, a steward was a household manager who handled finances for the owner. A steward was entrusted with the care of an owner's or a master's property, delegated to act on behalf of the master's interests. The modern equivalent might be the role of a manager or agent. But today, many people have little understanding of what it means to be a steward. Contemporary people may be familiar with wine stewards or stewards as attendants on boats or airplanes. The church so regularly uses stewardship as a code word for giving appeals or a blanket term for church finances that many hear it as nothing more than a thinly veiled euphemism for fundraising. But the belief that a Christian's role regarding money and possessions is that of a steward is profoundly relevant to how we understand our relationship to God and how we make decisions in our lives and churches.

From the very beginning, the Bible teaches that humankind's role in relation to God is that of a steward. In the opening chapters of Genesis, God plants a garden and places Adam and Eve there to till and keep it, with specific commands as to how they were to use it. And when they misuse it, there is a price to be paid. Later in Genesis, Joseph becomes a steward in Potiphar's household and later in Pharaoh's court. Exercising his responsibilities wisely, he protects Egypt from famine and reunites his own family, carrying forward God's promise.

In the New Testament, several of Jesus's parables relate to the role of a steward. In Luke 16:1–13, we find the story of a steward who is summoned before his master for squandering his property. Faced with the dilemma of how to provide for himself after his dismissal, he goes to his master's debtors and settles their accounts for a fraction of what is owed. And surprisingly, the master commends his shrewdness. In the parable of the talents (Matthew 25:14–30), Jesus tells the story of a man who entrusts his property to three individuals before going on a journey. One receives five talents and trades them to make five more. When called to account upon the master's return, the master commends him and puts him in charge of many things. Another receives two talents. He also returns double to the master and is commended. The third individual receives one talent. He is so afraid of losing the talent and incurring the master's rage that he buries it the ground. When the master returns, he derides this individual for failing to invest the talent profitably and denounces him as wicked and lazy. The talent is taken from him and given to the first individual who invested the five talents more fruitfully. Think what you will about the ultimate message of these parables. They fall into the category of parables that New Testament readers often find troubling or difficult. But they do tell us a great deal about the responsibilities of a steward.

In these Bible stories, we learn that stewards have a great deal of authority, autonomy, and responsibility. We learn that the role of steward can be an extremely powerful role, as it was for Joseph. We also learn that an effective steward must employ a good deal of creativity, initiative, and entrepreneurship in managing the master's affairs because a steward is expected to do well by the master. There is risk. And there is an expectation of fruitfulness.

But perhaps most importantly, we learn that a steward is accountable to the master. As stewards of God, we are subservient to God and responsible to God for our actions and the outcomes of our decisions.

STEWARDSHIP AND CHRISTIAN DISCIPLESHIP

What does this mean for our life of faith? If we take seriously the notion that everything we have comes from God and must be administered faithfully on God's behalf, then we must function as stewards in the household of God. This is true for both individual Christians, for congregations, and for the whole body of Christ. A simple working definition of Christian stewardship is: *Stewardship is about how we care for the things that God has entrusted to us in ways that serve God's purposes.* While the focus of this book is financial stewardship, this definition acknowledges that our responsibility as stewards extends to all the resources and responsibilities that God entrusts to us. It includes how we care for creation and the environment, how we manage our health and respect our bodies, and how we tend and nurture our relationships and families. Stewardship is a primary dimension of Christian faithfulness. It is a decision-making construct for how we employ our time, energy, and resources and how we purposefully orient our very selves. But this broader understanding should never dilute the fact that stewardship *is* about money and possessions and it *is* about how we support the church.

God has entrusted other responsibilities to us as well—to be the church, to bear the gospel message, and to carry forth God's mission in the world. Returning to Scripture, the concept of stewardship takes on a much larger meaning in the Epistles. Early church leaders expanded the notion of stewardship, borrowed from the ancient economic world, and used it as a lens for understanding our spiritual responsibilities as church leaders and recipients of God's love and grace. For example, 1 Peter 4:10 instructs us to be "good stewards of the manifold grace of God." A good Christian steward is a servant and agent of the gospel.

Unfortunately, talk of stewardship in the church often has a negative tone—not just because we don't like hearing about money and giving but also because it's unpleasant to be reminded of our responsibilities. But being God's stewards is a privilege and an opportunity, not a burden. As stewards, we serve as God's agents in the world. We become partners in God's mission through the church. Our giving to support the church is an essential, vital component of our overall stewardship. But stewardship can never be reduced to just that. As God's agents, we are called to live purposeful lives of accountable discipleship. The role of steward is an empowering role.

Faithful stewardship is part and parcel of a life of Christian discipleship. Understanding ourselves as stewards helps us acknowledge God's sovereignty and move from a me-centered to a God-centered way of being. Stewardship is a privilege that allows us to give tangible witness to our faith and our priorities. Ultimately, stewardship is about love of God and neighbor over self. The credibility of our Christian witness is at stake in the decisions we make about how to use the gifts God has given us.

Like the doctrine of the generosity of God, the doctrine of Christian stewardship is often misused and distorted. We conscribe its profound implications when we use the term stewardship as a mere catchphrase for the paradigm of voluntary giving in churches. And we delude ourselves when we think our responsibility as stewards applies only to the portion of resources we dedicate to the church, leaving us free to do as we please with the rest. The challenge of revitalizing the church today requires a bold, robust understanding of stewardship that reclaims what the Bible teaches—that God expects us to use the things entrusted to us to serve God's purposes in the world. As we turn to a discussion of financial management for individuals and congregations, this understanding of stewardship is the theological lens that guides us.

Chapter 8

Stewardship of Personal Finances

Getting one's own affairs in order is the first responsibility of a Christian steward. This may seem self-interested or even selfish. But it's a bit like the airline safety announcement reminding passengers to secure their own air masks before assisting others. People with insufficient financial resources or those who mismanage their resources are unable to respond adequately to God's call to generosity. Moreover, believing that God lovingly provides for our needs, we align ourselves with God's purposes when we exercise prudence in caring for our needs and those of our households. Yet many people at all income levels struggle with their finances due to a lack of basic financial management skills.

THREE REALMS OF PERSONAL FINANCIAL STEWARDSHIP

Three different realms of resources and responsibility pertain to personal finances. The first involves income and expenses. The second involves long-term needs and accumulated assets. And the third involves lifetime concerns and assets. Good stewardship requires attention to each of these categories. Yet many people focus almost exclusively on managing income and expenses, giving insufficient attention to longer-term concerns.

Income and Expenses

The first step in mastering personal finances is to take stock of regular income or cash flow—money that comes into a household on a regular basis. For many people it is their wages or salary. But it might include public benefits, child support, rental income, investment income, pension checks, Social Security benefits, or other retirement income. On the other side of the balance sheet are regular, ongoing expenses—rent or mortgage payments, groceries, household needs, clothing, childcare or child support, transportation, insurance and healthcare premiums, credit card payments or other debts, and taxes. While these basic elements of budgeting may seem obvious, many people live day by day, paycheck to paycheck, paying the most pressing bills without taking stock of the bigger picture.

Being a good steward in this first realm involves establishing a household budget, managing banking accounts, avoiding or minimizing debt, and establishing savings goals and plans. Controlling expenses is critical, but so too is adequate income. For some people, getting a sound financial footing may involve taking on additional work, pursuing a higher-paying job through training or professional development, or getting connected with available benefits. We recall John Wesley's famous admonition: "Earn all you can. Save all you can. Give all you can." You can't save or give what you don't earn. This maxim also reminds us that managing income and expenses is only the first rung on the ladder of individual stewardship. But this first, critical step positions us to plan for long-term needs and participate in God's mission through giving.

Long-Term Needs and Accumulated Assets

Good personal stewardship goes beyond just paying the monthly bills. It also involves planning for long-term needs, such as purchasing a home, paying for college, and planning for retirement. And as individuals devote resources toward these longer-term goals, they accumulate assets—savings, investments, equity in a home or other property, retirement accounts, life insurance policies, and so forth. Just as income is a resource to steward and manage in accordance with God's purposes, the same is true of accumulated assets.

Lifetime Needs and Assets

Sound personal stewardship also considers what happens when our life comes to an end. For anyone with minor children or other dependents, the preeminent concern is ensuring their financial security and care. One should also make provisions for final expenses so as not to burden survivors. After attending to these responsibilities, the question becomes how to dispense with what remains—generally any accumulated assets (savings, investments, real estate, personal property, retirement accounts, etc.) plus the proceeds of life insurance policies or other death benefits. Everyone needs a basic will specifying how they want their property and assets distributed. And a Christian steward considers how lifetime assets might also sustain a legacy of faith.

THREE PILLARS OF GIVING

When it comes to giving and tithing, most people only consider their income. But if we are called to give in proportion to what we have, accumulated assets and lifetime assets must also be factored into the equation. Clif Christopher refers to the three realms of personal finance as "three pockets of giving."[1] Few people think about making gifts from accumulated or lifetime assets and churches seldom think to ask. But a comprehensive understanding of financial stewardship considers God's claim not just on what we *earn* but also what we *own*. And in the next chapter we will see how giving from all three pillars provides different streams of income that correspond with a congregation's operating, capital, and permanent fund needs.

THE MINISTRY OF FINANCIAL LITERACY

If sound management of personal finances is the first responsibility of a Christian steward, then churches have a key role to play in educating, supporting, and equipping members for this task. Churches constantly ask their members to consider the church's financial situation but seldom offer to help members with their own financial challenges. But if everything entrusted to us belongs to God and is to be used in accordance with God's purposes, personal finances and spending decisions are as much a part of Christian discipleship as giving to the church. So, a ministry of financial education is a form of spiritual guidance. It is also a critical form of pastoral care that helps people with real-life concerns—meeting their family's basic needs, getting out from under the burden of educational or consumer debt, planning for retirement and healthcare needs, and estate planning.

Additionally, when churches help people better manage their resources, they become more generous. A study of operating practices in United Church of Canada congregations found that the churches experiencing growth in giving were four times more likely than other churches to offer some kind of personal financial instruction. And, the churches providing financial training had per capita giving 25 percent above the national average, and the increase in their per capita giving was 11 percent above the national average.[2] It stands to reason that those who think more deeply and more often about the connection between faith and finances will give more generously. And those empowered to manage expenses and avoid debt are certainly in a better position to give.

But spiritual and pastoral care, *not* enhancing church revenues, should be the primary goals of a financial literacy ministry. If the church's bottom line is the motivation, people will see right through it and fail to engage.

Congregations can minister to the financial concerns of members in many different ways. They must first answer some key questions. What needs are present in the congregation? Is the church located in a struggling community? A middle-class neighborhood? An affluent area? Are there young adults just getting started? Families with children? Or aging Baby Boomers and retirees? Most churches likely have a mix, of course. But basic budgeting and financial management might be more important in a younger or less affluent church, with retirement and estate planning more relevant in an older, more affluent church.

Creating support groups for people facing similar challenges is a simple way to understand concerns and provide guidance. Congregations can bring together those who are unemployed or in career transition, parents figuring out how to pay for college, or families struggling with medical expenses so they can resource and support one another. This approach doesn't require a great degree of expertise, but it helps to have some people in these groups who have successfully navigated the challenges and can facilitate connections with external resources.

Another simple homegrown option is to invite people from your congregation or community with financial expertise (bankers, financial planners, trust and estate lawyers, etc.) to lead workshops or seminars. It is essential, however, that these experts come with a desire to help others, not to sell their own services. Some congregations host an annual "ducks in a row" session focused on end-of-life planning—not just wills and estates, but also health directives and making sure essential records are accessible and in good order.

Congregations looking for a more comprehensive, structured approach to financial education can explore commercially available study curricula, video resources, and comprehensive training modules. The most basic programs tend to address spending, budgeting, savings, and debt, while more comprehensive programs also cover more advanced and long-term concerns. Congregations investing in these resources should first research carefully the costs, content, and spiritual perspective.

CLERGY PERSONAL FINANCES

For clergy, mastering personal finances is both a personal and a pastoral responsibility. It is often said, "You can't lead others where you haven't been yourself." When clergy model responsible personal stewardship and generous giving practices, they are better able to equip and encourage others.

Additionally, basic financial literacy skills lay a foundation for the work of church budgeting and financial management. As one seminary student put it, "If I can keep a budget, then I can instruct the church to keep a budget."[3] Yet too many clergy are ill-equipped and struggle with their own finances.

Clergy face all the same issues that parishioners do, but some require special attention for clergy. Budgeting is often complicated for clergy because of their relatively low salaries, especially clergy serving small membership churches. Yet even though the financial challenges of these clergy can be great, they may be better off than many of their congregants. When that is the case, depending on an increasing salary may be problematic. On the expense side, clergy increasingly carry significant educational debt due to the length of their education and modest starting salaries.

Accumulating savings and assets for family educational expenses and retirement is another critical issue for clergy, especially for clergy that live much of their lives in church-owned housing. Those living in parsonages avoid rent or mortgage payments, typically the largest monthly expense for other individuals or families. And they also avoid the significant costs of keeping up a home. But the flip side is that these clergy often enter retirement without what is generally the largest asset of a retiree—a home that is paid for—at just the same time they must enter the housing market for the first time. Currently, the U.S. tax code provides for clergy (and the military) a housing benefit when it comes to federal taxes. Clergy living in church-owned housing need to use this benefit to save for the time when they must provide their own housing.

In matters of personal finance, clergy are held to a high standard—not because they are clergy but because they are leaders. And no leader can be effective unless their personal stewardship reflects the values and commitments they espouse. Church members do not expect clergy to be perfect or immune from the financial challenges of their circumstances. But they do expect integrity, accountability, and honesty.

Chapter 9

Stewardship of Congregational Resources

Just as individual Christians are called to steward their personal finances wisely, congregations also must manage resources wisely to achieve their God-given mission. Churches exist solely to carry out their mission. And time and money are given exclusively to support things that make the mission a reality in the lives of members and the community. So missional imperatives should guide every financial decision.

But a church's mission is not a mission for just us and our moment as leaders. We are stewards of a mission that has been nurtured over years and often centuries. If the mission is worthy for us and our time, surely it is worthy to be continued for others in the future. Church leaders, therefore, must always focus on how best to fulfill today's mission in ways that do not compromise that mission in the future. In the business world, leaders are guided by the bottom line of profitability. The church does not have one bottom line, certainly not a purely financial one. But you can make the case that church finances should be evaluated by two bottom lines: mission and sustainability.

Congregational survival is not a worthy goal. Mission sustainability is. Mission achievement and financial sustainability are inextricably linked. Indeed, financial sustainability is how we achieve mission sustainability. A church's every decision usually impacts both sides of the coin. Our faith simply does not support a dichotomy between body and soul, which would allow us to focus on the spiritual as if it has no connection to material considerations. A Catholic nun who leads a large Catholic hospital puts it well when she said, "No margin, no mission."[1]

THE THREE FUNDS

Churches can ensure a solid financial foundation worthy of the importance of their mission by using three different funds to manage their resources—an operating fund, a capital renewal and replacement fund, and an endowment fund. An operating fund is essential. No church could exist without operating revenue. A capital renewal and replacement fund is equally essential if a congregation owns any facilities, yet not all churches have a capital fund. And an endowment fund is the least present in congregations. Some churches regard an endowment as a luxury or even a detriment. Yet a well-planned and managed endowment fund can enhance a church's ministry in the present while at the same time ensuring its long-term sustainability (see appendix A, for succinct descriptions of the three funds in a form easily usable with church leaders).

Operating Fund

The Bible says before building a tower one must "count the cost." An operating budget is the instrument congregations use to calculate the cost of deploying their mission year to year. When most people think of a church budget, the operating budget is what they have in mind.

- The *purpose* of the operating budget is to cover the annual operating needs.
- The *goal* of the operating budget is to ensure that the church fulfills its mission and vision in the coming year in ways consistent with the church's values and the future sustainability of the congregation.
- The *defining characteristic* of the operating budget is that it pays expenses incurred and used within the year through recurring and predictable income.

The operating budget should be funded by recurring and relatively predictable sources of income such as pledges, offerings, a portion of rental income, program and user fees, fundraisers, and other ongoing revenue sources. Churches should avoid funding their operating budgets with nonrecurring and unpredictable sources such as bequests, spending from an endowment at too high a rate, using reserve funds for routine deficits rather than specific emergencies, or onetime unexpected gifts. Using these nonrecurring sources of revenue for operations simply delays the day when the gap between recurring income and recurring expenses must be addressed. Income from these nonrecurring sources can be used more fruitfully for the capital fund or endowment.

Capital Fund

When Jesus said, "Which of you, intending to build a tower, does not first sit down and estimate the cost?" (Luke 14:28), he could also have added that once you build the tower, be prepared for upkeep costs! Just as church leaders give careful oversight to annual operational needs, they also need to provide for longer-term capital needs. By establishing a capital or building budget, churches can plan for long-term facility needs and dedicate certain income sources to meet these needs.

- The *purpose* of a capital budget is to fund new building, renovation, and major repairs and replacement.
- The *goal* of capital budgeting is to ensure that the church's property, facilities, and equipment are adequate to achieve the mission and are kept safe, accessible, and up to date through an ongoing review and renewal plan.
- The *defining characteristic* of the capital budget is that it covers capital projects with a life longer than one year. Some churches define a capital expense by its costs, for example, any project that costs $1,000 or more.

It would be a mistake to think about the operating budget as dealing with ministry and the capital budget as addressing facilities. Both budgets are shaped totally by your church's mission. Remember that every dollar given to your church becomes part of the shared assets of the congregation to be used to advance its mission.[2] This is a characteristic of a "commonwealth" congregation. Commonwealth is a concept used by James Hudnut-Beumler to describe how a congregation uses all of its financial and physical assets for one purpose only, the common mission of the church.[3] Because of the constant pressure to meet operating budgets, churches often act as if they have no capital expenses and continually defer necessary maintenance. Then, when such expenses come along in the form of a leaking roof or a furnace that must be replaced, they have to resort to emergency appeals or draw from the operating budget and throw the church into the red for the year.

Churches can fund a capital budget by designating a percentage of the operating budget to be transferred to this fund each year. Special gifts, memorials, bequests, fundraisers, and the proceeds of property sales are other possible sources of capital funds. Major capital needs or building projects are often funded through a special capital campaign or by borrowing funds.

Endowment or Permanent Fund

- The *purpose* of an endowment is to provide a continuing source of funding for the church through invested permanent funds.

- The *goal* of an endowment is to receive gifts and bequests that are maintained on a long-term basis to support the church's mission into the future.
- The *defining characteristic* of an endowment is that the value of the principal is preserved and earnings (interest, dividends, and appreciation) are available for purposes established by the congregation or designated by the donor and accepted by the congregation.

Some churches are reluctant to establish an endowment fund for fear that it will decrease giving. But if an endowment is handled properly, this potential pitfall can be avoided. An endowment can play a role in an overall plan for funding operations, but it should never be an excuse for members not to support the budget adequately or a subsidy for shortfalls. Bequests are the primary source of endowment funds in most churches. Other sources include special designated gifts, memorials, sale of property (particularly if it is a parsonage where the principal will be needed to fund a housing allowance), larger onetime gifts, and reinvested appreciation of endowment funds.

THE THREE FUNDS AND THE THREE PILLARS OF GIVING

There is a natural symmetry between the three realms of resources pertaining to individual stewardship and a congregation's three funds. When a congregation organizes its finances according to these three categories, it can promote a well-balanced giving program that encourages members to give out of their three pockets of giving—income, accumulated assets, and lifetime assets. Tithes and offerings are generally given out of an individual's regular income or cash flow. They are the primary source of income for a church's operating expenses. Major gifts from accumulated assets are a primary source of funding for a church's capital expenses. And bequests or other gifts of lifetime assets are the primary source of funding for a church's endowment or permanent fund.

Regularly receiving gifts from all three pillars provides different streams of income that correspond with a congregation's operating, capital, and permanent fund needs. Yet churches tend to put almost all of their emphasis on encouraging people to give out of the first pocket of giving—income. The only time most churches even think about seeking gifts from accumulated assets is when they need a new building. Even then, most churches do this reluctantly. Similarly, very few churches intentionally encourage their members to think about the stewardship of the assets they will leave behind. According to a recent tally, religious causes received 31 percent of all charitable donations in the United States.[4] However, as Clif Christopher points out,

Three Pillars of Giving

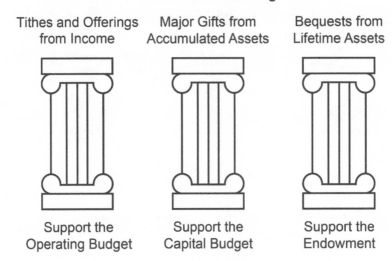

| Tithes and Offerings from Income | Major Gifts from Accumulated Assets | Bequests from Lifetime Assets |

Support the Operating Budget · Support the Capital Budget · Support the Endowment

only 8 percent of estate gifts go to churches and the estate gifts they receive are smaller than the gifts to other causes.[5] This is not because people don't care about their churches. It's because their churches haven't been deliberate in teaching about the stewardship of one's lifetime assets. In the chapters that follow on capital budgets and endowments, we will consider how churches can give more priority to encouraging major gifts and bequests.

Chapter 10

Building and Funding an Operating Budget

Developing an operating budget is not a chore but an opportunity to clarify the church's mission, discern what God is calling the church to do in the next year, and formulate plans to accomplish those goals. Remember, everything given to a congregation is to be used by the church only for the advancement of its mission. Since financial resources are always limited, planning a budget forces a congregation to make choices. Budgeting is a genuinely spiritual activity that helps a church clarify its heart and assure that its treasure follows.

While financial leaders can guide the process, they need prayer, discernment, and input from a range of congregational leaders. Your denominational polity and your church's decision-making processes will shape how your budget is approved. But the engagement of other church leaders is needed long before the formal approval of a final budget. Before developing a budget, the finance committee should seek clarity from the congregation on some fundamental questions.

- *What is God's purpose for our church?* If your church doesn't have a clear sense of purpose, this is a wonderful time to revisit this question.
- *What is the next faithful step to which God calls us now?* While a church's purpose may stay the same year to year, circumstances change. So ask what God would have you do in the coming year, given the current realities in your church and in your community.
- *What are the values we want to honor in all we do?* Values don't precede purpose because you may honor values perfectly yet not accomplish God's purpose for your church. However, clarifying your core values provides guidance and boundaries for carrying out your purpose and gives a standard for ensuring the values you profess are honored in your plans.

When you have clarified your purpose, next faithful step, and core values, you are ready to ask: *What plans need to be made to implement what we believe God is calling us to do?* For example, if you believe God is calling the church to focus especially on children, what plans are needed to make that happen? Before formulating a budget that can support this vision, different leaders in the church need to come to a consensus on plans and programs to move this goal forward.

STUDY RECENT FINANCIAL HISTORY

Another preliminary step is to review recent financial history. When it comes to finances, the best predictor of the future is the recent past. This doesn't mean major changes can't occur. But changes tend to occur incrementally, not suddenly, so your budget should be informed by how well budgets in recent years matched actual income and expenses as well as trends in revenue, giving, and pledging. These comparisons should inform your projections for the next year's budget.

Budget History

Completing the budget history chart shown in table 10.1 will reveal how budget estimates for the past several years compare with actual income and expenses. What patterns do you observe? In years with a net surplus, was it due to higher income or lower-than-expected expenses? In years with a deficit, was it due to reduced income or higher-than-expected expenses? Is the gap growing larger each year? Pay attention to the trends. Churches commonly receive less money than they project in their budgets, but they also tend to spend less as well.

Revenue History

The revenue history chart shown in table 10.2 is helpful in assessing the relative importance of different sources of income in recent years. After

Table 10.1 Budget History

	20XX	20XX	20XX	20XX	20XX
Budgeted income					
Actual income					
More (less)					
Budgeted expenses					
Actual expenses					
More (less)					
Net surplus (deficit)					

Table 10.2 Revenue History

Sources of income	20XX	20XX	20XX	20XX	20XX
Tithes and offerings					
Other contributions					
Rental income					
Wedding and other user fees					
Fundraisers					

Table 10.3 Recent Pledging History

	20XX	20XX	20XX	20XX	20XX
Budget	$	$	$	$	$
Amount pledged	$	$	$	$	$
# of pledging units					
Total given (pledged and unpledged)	$	$	$	$	$
Pledged as percentage of total given	%	%	%	%	%

identifying the primary sources of your operating funds, take note of which sources are becoming more significant and which are declining.

Pledging Patterns

Not all churches rely on pledging or estimates of giving, but many do. If you do, you will want to calculate what percentage of your total giving comes from pledges. The recent pledging history chart illustrated in table 10.3 permits you to see the trends in several components of pledging with the final being what percentage your pledges represent of the total giving from all sources (not just from pledges). These figures can help project more reliably the income you might expect in the coming year based on the pledges received. Remember that the relationship between the amount pledged and total giving varies significantly from church to church. If you discover, for example, that the amount pledged is typically 80 percent of the actual income from all sources, this gives a basis to estimate your total giving in future years based on the amount pledged. You may discover that patterns are shifting. If changes are taking place, you need to be aware of the direction of the changes.

DIFFERENT MODELS FOR BUILDING A BUDGET

What process should you use to draft your annual operating budget? Churches commonly employ these different approaches, each with advantages and disadvantages.

Begin with a Blank Slate

Beginning with a blank slate is often called zero-based budgeting because you disregard the amounts budgeted in past years and build a budget back from scratch. This approach is motivated by the laudatory goal of freeing the budget from the shackles of the past, but it is extremely time-consuming and rarely accomplishes what people hope it will. Even after spending all the time and effort to rebuild a budget from the ground up, the new budget typically looks amazingly similar to the previous budget.

Begin with Last Year's Budget

It is relatively easy to begin with last year's budget. You simply compare the income and expense lines in the past year's budget with actual income and expenses. Then you make changes based on that history and other anticipated changes. For example, if the church didn't spend as much on postage last year, that line item is reduced for the coming year. Or if utilities were more than projected, that line item is increased. You ask your insurance company for an estimated cost for the coming year. Then account for any recommended increases in salaries or denominational commitments. This approach is simple, though it rarely leads to changes in priorities or new initiatives. Smaller churches typically rely on this model.

Begin with Budget Requests

Some churches begin by asking all ministry areas or administrative units to submit budget requests. You ask some person or group responsible for every section of the budget to describe their plans for the next year and submit a budget request based on their anticipated needs. This model is commonly used in midsize and larger churches.

Begin with a New Overarching Vision

When the church begins budgeting by asking what faithful step God is calling them to take next, the answer is usually incremental enough to fit the current direction of the church. There are, however, moments in a church's history when business as usual is not enough. This doesn't mean starting over or changing everything. But it does mean there is such a pressing challenge or opportunity that a new vision is needed to direct all ministries toward the new reality. This new vision must become the "invisible leader"[1] that guides all planning.

For example, a church may discover that the average age in the congregation has increased every year for twenty years while the average age in the community has decreased and grade school enrollment is growing. Merely improving the church's shut-in ministry or expanding their food pantry hours will not address their situation. In their planning, a vision emerges around reaching younger people. The usual next steps would be to name a task group and add some funds for it in the budget. Such a plan will fail. The church should instead ask every ministry of the church to make plans that contribute to this vision. Instead of asking groups for a budget request, you ask them to plan a ministry that will allow them to reach a constituency somewhat younger than the one they currently reach. This planning becomes the basis for preparing a new budget.

Begin with Income Projections

In this model you project income from all sources based on trends and other data. You look at three things: trends over the past three or four years, what you see happening in the current year, and anything already known about the coming year. Perhaps a source of income for the past several years is no longer available, or you know income from another source will go up. You take these factors into account. And these income projections set the parameters for building the budget.

A variant of this model is to wait until all pledges for the coming year are submitted and then build the budget around the pledge total. This doesn't mean you only budget for the income pledged. If, for example, pledges typically amount to about 80 percent of the total contributed by all givers (pledgers and others), and that ratio has been fairly consistent over recent years, you would add an additional 20 percent to account for non-pledge giving in calculating your total contributions income.

Rarely is one of these models sufficient by itself. Realities normally require combining several of these approaches with a dynamic interplay between the estimates produced by any of these plans and other financial limits or ministry needs. For example, when groups are asked to submit their budgets and their requests are compared to projected revenues, you may realize there is a gap between needs and anticipated income. If that happens, there must be a back-and-forth to adjust plans. That kind of interplay is quite common and very helpful in producing a budget that is challenging but also realistic. In the end, you want a budget that projects a challenging vision but doesn't deal in fantasies. You don't want a budget total so large that no matter how hard everyone works, or how much people give, failure is a given from the beginning. On the other hand, you don't want the budget to be so modest and unchallenging that it will not stretch congregants' giving.

OPERATING BUDGET EXPENSE CATEGORIES

Churches organize their expenses in various ways. The most common categories include personnel, missions, program, and facilities. When crafting an operational budget, the following expense categories can be helpful. But every congregation needs to come up with a scheme that fits its unique needs, program, and practices.

Personnel

Clergy salaries, benefits, and housing are the most significant personnel expenses for most congregations, certainly for those with one hundred or fewer in worship. As churches grow larger, the number of paid lay staff grows and represents a higher percentage of personnel expenses. Churches with 1,000 or more in attendance will normally spend far more on lay staff than clergy. Personnel expenses normally include not only salary, benefits, and payroll taxes but also travel, continuing education, and other out-of-pocket expenses for clergy and possibly other staff.

Facilities

Expenses related to providing physical space to house the congregation's activities are generally the next biggest area of expense—mortgage payments or rent, utility bills, property insurance, cleaning, landscaping, routine upkeep expenses, and so forth. Building maintenance is a major expense for many congregations, particularly those with older facilities. In the next chapter we discuss how a capital budget can be used to account for building expenses with a lifespan of more than one year. Operating budget expenses for facilities, together with capital budget expenditures for capital renewal and replacement, represent a church's total expenditures for facilities, even though only a portion may be included in the operating budget.

Programs

Program expenses support the internal activities of a congregation—worship, education, evangelism, music, children's and youth activities, adult programs, special events, and so forth. These are the ministries that reach new disciples and help current members to grow in their discipleship and spiritual development.

Missions and Benevolences

For many congregations, their mission support begins with their support of denominational initiatives through some type of apportioned or "fair share" giving. Nondenominational churches practice such giving normally through networks or associations or parachurch organizations. Building on that contribution, churches support a myriad of serving ministries in their communities, their nation, and the world. There may sometimes seem to be overlap between mission and programs, but mission expenditures are generally thought of as programs that serve an external constituency. Ask whether the money is going for those inside or outside your congregation.

The percentage spent for each expense category varies dramatically across congregations based on size, demographics, and polity. However, there are some patterns that may give clues for your church. In their recent study of congregations' economic practices, the Lake Institute found that congregations in the United States across religious traditions on average spend 49 percent on personnel; 23 percent on facilities; 17 percent on missions; and 10 percent on program.[2] A Lewis Center analysis of 2016 spending by United Methodist congregations revealed these percentages: 45.8 percent on personnel; 31.7 percent on facilities (includes operating and capital budgets); 14.8 percent on missions; and 7.7 percent on program.

Cash Reserves

While not always thought of or included as an expense category, a church needs a cash reserve account with policies about its size and use. There should be a goal for the size of the reserve fund based on some objective standard. The goal may be to maintain a reserve that is equivalent of three months or six months operating expenses. Policies for its use are similar to the way a family might use an emergency fund. It is for a financial need that could not be anticipated when the budget was set. It could be a recession, the closing of a large employer in the community, or a legal judgment against the church. These reserve funds may also serve as a source to meet cash flow during certain times of the year. Resist the temptation to underfund or overfund the reserve. You should have policies about how the reserve is funded until it reaches its goal and what to do when the fund needs to be replenished or drawn down once the goal is reached. Any additional surplus funds need a better use than building up the reserve beyond necessity.

OPERATING BUDGET INCOME SOURCES

The person not involved with church finances probably sees the collection plate passed in worship and thinks the offerings are the only source of church income. But most churches rely on multiple streams of income. Keep in mind this important principle: funding for the operating budget should come from *recurring and predictable* sources of income. You don't want to depend on income that doesn't come every year to pay annual expenses. So, for example, it's generally unwise to use undesignated bequests for operational purposes. Using such nonrecurring or unpredictable income for operating expenses simply sets the church up for failure later. There are better ways to use those unexpected funds. Predictable income doesn't mean you know the exact source of every dollar. For example, you might have a line in the budget for fees from groups that use facilities. You know that amount has averaged about $3,000 a year for the past five years, so you budget $3,000 without knowing from whom every fee will come. That is still predictable income. This is a reasonable approach to estimating many predictable income streams.

Contributions and Gifts

Pledges or Estimates of Giving

Many churches ask members to make pledges or estimates of giving annually. For these churches, pledge payments typically constitute the largest portion of their operating income.

Other Giving by Members and Participants

Even in churches with a strong tradition of annual pledging, there are always persons who do not pledge but give regularly. Many may be some of the most active participants. Donations from members and constituents who do not pledge is an increasing percentage of total gifts in some churches where the number of pledgers is declining but the number of givers is not. This trend was identified in the aftermath of the 2008 economic downturn.

Giving by Visitors

Many churches do not know how much income they get each year from those visiting their congregations. It is a sad fact that if someone visiting and making a gift to your church, perhaps out-of-town guests attending with local family members, the first acknowledgment of that gift is made the next January when contribution statements are sent for tax purposes. Visitor gifts may not be a significant source of income in your church, but you won't know until you check. Spend some time monitoring such gifts (and thanking the givers) and you will know.

Church School Offerings, Communion Offerings, or Special Offerings

This may include special offerings taken on holidays or anniversaries or special appeals for specific projects or missions. Increasingly, the Christmas Eve offering is becoming significant in many churches.

Memorial Donations and Honor Gifts

It is often the custom for the family and friends of deceased church members to make gifts to the congregation in memory of the person who has died. Where cultivated and acknowledged promptly and appropriately, these gifts contribute regularly to the income of many churches.

Other Income Streams

Rental Income

Rental income is often used in operating budgets. But it is a mistake to use 100 percent of rental income for operations. Most rental income is better used for the capital budget to offset the heavy wear and tear on facilities incurred by renters.

Day Care or Preschool Income

Churches have varying arrangements with preschool or day care programs operating in their buildings. In some churches, these fall under the rental income category since the program is operated by an external entity. When the program belongs to the church, there are still varying financial arrangements. Sometimes the programs are subsidized by the church's operating budget, thus becoming an expense for budgeting purposes. Other programs "break even," though often only calculating direct out-of-pocket expenses and not staff time by those not compensated by the program. Chapter 17 addresses rental income and gives ideas for calculating the expenses for these programs, whether run by the church or someone else.

User Fees

Many churches charge fees for certain events such as weddings or the occasional use of some portion of the church facilities. Churches may also collect fees for study materials, youth outings, or other activities. Churches need to assess whether such fees limit participation. Some churches may believe that a modest registration fee for Vacation Bible School would make no different in attendance while other churches would know that participation would be sharply curtailed by any fee no matter how small.

Other Sources of Funds

Fundraisers

Fundraisers are a mainstay of the economic model for some churches. Other churches discourage or restrict fundraisers. If you use fundraisers, pay careful attention to the cost/benefit ratio. Fundraisers are often not a very efficient way to raise money and they can sap so much energy that they detract from other ministry efforts. But some fundraisers do make financial sense and they can build camaraderie as people work together.

Endowment Income

Some churches use income from endowments to fund their operations. Caution is in order, but under some circumstances it is appropriate—for example, when endowment funds are given to support distinctive ministry areas such as music or youth. In those cases, this portion of the endowment income can be used in the operating budget to offset those expenses. Let's say a gift was given to endow the church's music ministry and the income derived from that gift is $2,000 this year. If your operating budget includes more than $2,000 for music, the endowment funds can contribute $2,000 toward those expenses.

Many churches use endowment earnings as a general subsidy for the operating budget. But this can become a crutch that discourages giving and prevents a church from coming to grips with the underlying financial realities. Earnings from endowments often are better spent on things that make the church stronger for the future rather than getting through today's expenses. Using endowment funds for things with a life of more than a year, such as capital projects, takes the long view and frees current member contributions for more ongoing ministries and mission.

Gifts in Kind

While not a gift that is recorded on the income ledger, gifts in kind function as income. Gifts in kind provide products or services that the church would otherwise cover by spending from the operating budget. For example, one church might have money in the budget for flowers, while another church has a sign-up list for members to bring flowers. Those providing the flowers weekly at their own expense are providing a gift in kind that otherwise would be paid by operating funds. Gifts in kind should not be a revenue category in your budget. But you should be aware of their impact on your operating expenses and consider whether additional gifts in kind might meet other needs.

OTHER CONSIDERATIONS

What If the Budget Doesn't Balance?

What if, despite your best efforts, you are still projecting more expense than income? If it is just a little different, it won't matter a lot, since usually not every line item is expended. If the gap is large, you need to work on a solution. If the proposed remedy is to draw from reserves, keep in mind that you are drawing from nonrecurring funds. An unbalanced budget signifies that the baseline provided by predictable and recurring income is out of kilter with recurring expenses. It's better to address that situation promptly and positively than to draw on other nonrecurring sources, especially for more than a year.

Communication

Communication is critical to building a budget from the very beginning of the process. Let people know what questions are being asked and how they can share ideas. Share information as your budget takes shape. Give opportunities for feedback. As you seek commitments and giving, report on how the budget is coming along. As an audit from the previous year is completed, make sure people know how to access it if they are interested.

God's stewards in the church have always been entrusted with using the faith community's resources fruitfully in service of God's purposes. As you plan and pray, always remember that seeking to accomplish God's purposes for your church in the coming year is always a process of spiritual discernment. When you ask what this mission will cost and what resources you have to accomplish it, you are doing holy work on behalf of a community of believers looking to you for competent and inspired leadership.

Chapter 11

Building and Funding a Capital Budget

When people think of church budgets, they usually have in mind the operating budget. The operating budget receives most of the attention since day-to-day ministries depend on it. But there is another budget equally important to the future of your congregation—the capital budget. Capital budgets go by different names. In some churches, the building fund serves as the capital budget. While churches use a variety of terms, it is important for all churches to ask two questions: Do we have an ongoing plan to address each year our capital renewal and replacement needs? And do we have sources of income that provide for these needs?

Unfortunately, when operating funds are scarce, as they frequently are in congregations, the first response is often to defer maintenance. After a few years of deferred maintenance, the capital needs accumulate to a size that seems impossible to address. Then a crisis comes when something major must be replaced, and there are no funds for even a portion of the cost. A capital budget is designed to avoid such an untenable situation.

THE CAPITAL BUDGET SERVES A CHURCH'S MISSION

It is important to focus on building needs through the lens of mission. If you think about your property and facilities as assets to fulfill the church's mission, it's easier to avoid focusing merely on bricks and mortar. For example, a congregation debated for a year about repainting the sanctuary. Two groups had opposite views on how the repainted sanctuary should look. Then one person asked a question that changed the conversation: "For whom are we painting the sanctuary?" That opened a missional way to think about the property. Our mission clarifies what facilities we need and how to make decisions about their use. Since the capital budget is about mission more than buildings, planning takes the same spiritual foundation of prayer, discernment, and preparation as the operating budget. And since all property, facilities, and equipment exist to carry out the church's mission, decisions cannot be made apart from how the congregation is seeking to fulfill God's mission. Those charged with oversight of the property, therefore, cannot begin their work without engaging many other church leaders in discerning the church's mission, needs, and future direction. Just as finance committees cannot develop an operating budget by themselves, trustees and property committees need to ask others for guidance on the missional direction of capital expenditures.

Begin by Engaging the Big Questions

All budgeting must keep in mind the same foundational questions: *What is God's purpose for our church? What is the next faithful step to which God is calling us now? And, what are the values we want to honor in all we do?* But capital budgeters have some more specific questions to ask before proceeding.

- *Why have facilities?* Asking such a question may seem silly and unnecessary, but it is a way to discuss quickly the purposes you see for your facilities. Some churches today choose not to have their own facilities, but the overwhelming majority do.
- *What facilities do we need for our mission, especially today's mission needs?* Be very specific. Define how many worshipers your worship space needs to accommodate, as well as the type of space needed for your current style of worship. How many classrooms, offices, and so forth, are needed, given today's realities? These needs are surely different than when the facility was built. How much greeting space is needed? Where are current goals and facilities most in and out of alignment?

- *What facilities do we have now and in what condition are they?* Long-established churches are often in buildings designed for the needs of a different era and with tremendous deferred maintenance needs. Asking if you have the right facilities is as important as inquiring about their condition. You may discover that some facilities (in varying conditions) are not particularly useful today; some facilities (in varying conditions) are very much needed today; some needs are unmet by current facilities; and some facilities can be repurposed.

Many church leaders should help answer these questions. Such conversations are not needed every year, but if you cannot remember the last time they were discussed, it's time to consider how best to direct this type of planning to advance the church's mission and goals. While such conversations can lead to unrealistic wish lists, trustees and property committees must sort out the most pressing and essential themes and concerns. Your goal is to be responsive, not reactive. As you report your plans and progress to church leaders, help them see how your efforts are clearly guided by the church's mission and the priorities they helped to establish.

ASSESSING THE CURRENT SITUATION

Condition of Facilities

Before developing a plan to address your current and future needs, you need a more detailed assessment of the condition of all aspects of your property and facilities. This can be something as simple as making a list of all the various areas of your facilities—sanctuary, narthex, restrooms, fellowship hall, grounds, parking, and so forth. Then prepare a rating system such as ☐Excellent condition; ☐Adequate for our needs; ☐Needs work; ☐Not acceptable.

Ask a number of different people to walk around and complete this survey on their own. Different people will see different things. Once the results are compiled, the big patterns will emerge.

Usage of Facilities

You need to know not only the condition of facilities but also current usage, which you can assess through a space usage study. Simply record how many people are using each of your rooms and spaces during each hour of the day during a typical two-week period. You will need to involve several people in this project to carry out the simple task of recording a number for each hour of the day for two weeks.

It may turn out that a space in bad condition is not used very much. You may be better off relocating the few people who use it than devoting precious capital dollars to renovating a rarely used space. Or you may discover a heavily used space is inadequate. Often churches think they need more space but discover they can accomplish their goals by using current space more efficiently or by repurposing existing square footage for different functions.

Preventive Maintenance Needs

Preventive maintenance should be an important part of your plan. A good preventive maintenance program can improve safety and extend the useful life of capital assets. Most preventive maintenance saves money in the long run by avoiding major repairs, decreasing equipment downtime, reducing the number of emergency maintenance calls, improving safety, and increasing the life expectancy of assets—perhaps up to five years or more for heating, ventilation, and air conditioning (HVAC) systems.

Environmental Stewardship

An environmental audit can also be useful. Steps taken to make your building eco-friendlier will also generally reduce operating costs. For example, one church had exit signs using 40-watt bulbs that needed to be changed two to four times a year. They replaced these with new signs using 2.9-watt LED lights. At their electricity rate, they saved almost $1,000 *per sign*. Another church was wasting electricity because lights were often left on. Installing motion-sensor lighting saved energy and money. A church in California installed solar panels in their parking lot which generated electricity for the church and provided shaded parking spaces.

ORGANIZING AND SETTING PRIORITIES

You are now ready to make a list of current and future needs. It will be a long list but, at this point, don't worry about the length. You are trying to capture a comprehensive picture of your needs.

Categories

The first step is to bring some order to this collection of projects. You will notice that the needs vary widely in subject, scope, urgency, and cost. Organize projects into categories such as health, safety, and code compliance; accessibility; major systems (heating and cooling, technology, and sound systems, etc.); equipment and furnishings; roofs; painting; renovation; and new construction (see appendix B for charts that will help you work through these steps).

Sequencing

Next, think about project sequencing. Prepare a chart with yearly columns extending five to ten years into the future and rows for your different categories and the needs identified in each. Place the highest priority projects in year one. Health, safety, and code compliance always come first. Next, divide large projects into units that can be spread across multiple years. Recurring projects such as painting and technology replacement can be done in increments over several years. None of this is exact or perfect, but you have to start somewhere. Be flexible. For example, if you expect that two roofs will need to be replaced in the next ten years, put this work on the schedule based on the current condition of the roofs. If it turns out that the roofs have more years of useful life than expected, reschedule roof replacement and work on other projects. There will *always* be other projects! Alternatively, if one of the roofs deteriorates faster than expected, replacing it will have to take precedence over a project that can be safely delayed.

Assign Costs and Set Goals

Once you have laid out your needs by year and category, you are ready for the truly hard part—counting the costs of all these projects. If someone saw your chart of capital needs organized by categories and years, they would surely be impressed. They might even think you have a capital renewal and replacement plan. In reality, you have a wish list. Tentative cost estimates need to be assigned to each project. Be prepared for the total to surprise you, and not in a good way. The key question now is, "What are the most pressing needs now and for the next one to three years and how do we begin addressing them?"

FUNDING YOUR CAPITAL BUDGET

One of the big mistakes most churches make is not having any ongoing sources of income that provide at least some basic funds for capital expenditures. So, it's important to consider possible income streams that might support your capital budget.

Capital Campaigns

The pattern for many churches is to address capital needs through a capital campaign or a similar fund drive. This is generally how churches fund construction, whether they are building a new church or extending an existing building. Increasingly, churches combine ongoing maintenance needs into a major renovation package funded by a campaign. But other funding sources are needed for more routine capital expenses.

Loans

Loans are often used to augment the proceeds of a capital campaign for new construction or other major projects. Sometimes smaller loans are used to finance unanticipated expenses, such as storm damage or major equipment replacement. Ideally, borrowing should be a small component of your capital plan, and loans will be short term rather than long term.

Funds Transferred from the Operating Budget

In addition to lines in their operating budget for basic maintenance and custodial expenses, many churches have a line that transfers money into the capital fund each month. Try to start such a transfer in your next budget, even if you have to start with a tiny percentage of the budget. If there are surplus operating funds at the end of the year, the capital fund is an excellent use for a portion of this money. It's helpful to have a policy to govern the use of any surplus. For example, some churches put half into the capital fund and use the remaining half as an emergency reserve for their operating budget.

Endowment or Permanent Fund

An endowment or other permanent income-producing fund can be a wonderful source of ongoing income for capital projects. It is one of the best uses of endowment earnings since most endowments come from planned gifts of lifetime assets. By using the earnings for capital projects, which generally have long lifespans, you extend the length of the donor's stewardship witness. Also, by taking care of these long-term issues, more money given by current members can be used for immediate ministry needs. Spending such funds on capital projects should also strengthen the church, help it remain vital in the future, and reach more people.

Rental Income and Building Use Fees

Rents and building use fees are a growing source of income for many churches. Often all of this income goes to the operating budget. But a much more appropriate policy is to divide this revenue between the operating and capital budgets. While building use incurs operating expenses, rentals place a large toll on facilities. This is particularly true when renting to childcare or preschool programs, which use the building heavily. Develop a reasonable formula that allocates some portion of rental income to the operating budget but a larger portion to the capital budget.

Gifts

Some people are particularly motivated to support capital needs, especially when making larger gifts. Bequests are a common source of capital funds, especially in churches that have a policy dedicating undesignated bequests, or some portion of undesignated bequests, to the capital fund. Other churches use all or a portion of memorial gifts not designated for some other purpose for capital needs.

Sale of Capital Assets

When a congregation sells a major asset, such as a building or a piece of property, it generally makes sense to dedicate the proceeds to the capital fund. Since this is a nonrecurring source of income, it is inadvisable to apply it to the operating budget.

Gifts in Kind

There may be people in the church who can support capital improvement projects through in-kind gifts—providing supplies or services for free or for a greatly reduced price. This can range from a business owner doing the work on a *pro bono* basis to a team of church volunteers providing free labor or a retired person volunteering to oversee the work.

Fundraisers

Churches often cover smaller capital expenses through fundraisers. Often, it is more effective to raise funds for a particular capital project than for the capital fund as a whole. But as with any other fundraising activities, you must carefully consider whether the amount of effort is worthwhile.

CAPITAL GIVING AND ENHANCED GENEROSITY

Pressing facility needs are often chronically underfunded because churches don't do enough to encourage capital giving. Many congregations are so daunted by the prospect of undertaking a capital campaign or seeking other major gifts that they fail to challenge their members to see themselves as stewards of the church's property. This not only contributes to poor stewardship of a congregation's physical plant; it also prevents church members from fully developing their own generosity. Remember, a well-balanced approach to giving encourages people to give from all three pockets of giving. And gifts from accumulated assets are a logical source of revenue for church capital needs.

The good news is that a capital campaign or other major gift initiative can be a positive experience that energizes a church and spurs greater generosity. Church members who stretch themselves to make major gifts often discover they can give more—and continue to do so. Additionally, some donors are particularly motivated to give to brick and mortar needs because they are tangible, easily communicated, and often of lasting value. Seeking capital gifts connects with those givers who have a deeply felt concern for facilities.

While it is typical to seek major gifts when constructing a new building or adding space, smaller capital needs or restoration projects can be equally appealing opportunities for giving. Seeking donations for some smaller capital projects is a great way to flex your congregation's major giving muscles, especially since many people are motivated to give in response to specific needs. When churches fail to ask members for this type of support, they generally lose out to other charities and nonprofits who aggressively seek major gifts.

Churches tend to do very well at understanding and meeting their current needs and implementing their current ministries. Churches do not do as well at looking ahead to long-term needs that are very predictable in many cases. Because of that, churches are often caught. Something breaks or wears out, and there are no funds available to meet the need. And then the church must rely on the only funds available—operating funds. Once that occurs, the finances for the entire year are disrupted. Being prudent and planning ahead are very important because facilities are part of your ministry.

Keep in mind that a capital budget is a guide or a blueprint that will change from year to year. Sometimes it must change within a year because of changed circumstances. No matter how well you do your work, there will be capital needs occurring for which you will not have adequate funds on hand. However, focusing on a capital budget will put you in a much better position to address more easily even the hardest situations.

Chapter 12

Building and Funding an Endowment

It is often said that the Christian faith is always only one generation away from extinction. Each of us stands on the shoulders of previous generations of Christian believers—those who nurtured our faith, who sacrificed to construct our buildings, who sustained the institutions that extend our witness. We, too, have a responsibility to the generations who will follow in our footsteps. An endowment is a vehicle that allows a church to set aside resources to ensure the vitality of its mission in the future. If you plan well and institute future-oriented policies, an endowment can be an important part of building a healthy financial future for your church.

There are many benefits to church endowment funds. An endowment allows individuals to extend the witness of their personal stewardship by contributing to something with lasting value and impact. Since endowments are typically funded through bequests that represent the accumulated wealth of one or more lifetimes, it is appropriate that these gifts create a lasting legacy. An endowment can also enhance a church's ability to sustain its mission, often supporting ministries that would not otherwise be possible. But there are potential downsides to endowments, as well. Using an endowment to cover chronic shortfalls can shield a church from having to adjust unrealistic or unsustainable operating budgets. And churches that become overly dependent on an endowment often fail to challenge their members to give adequately in relation to the church's actual needs. Spending too much from an endowment diminishes its future potential and compromises its ultimate purpose. To avoid these pitfalls, churches need to be clear about the purpose of an endowment and enact policies that ensure the proper management and use of endowment funds.

TYPES OF ENDOWMENTS

Endowment funds are different from other church funds in that they are set aside permanently, either by the donor or the church-governing body. There are, however, some major differences in the types of funds that serve as endowment.

True and Quasi-Endowment Funds

True endowment funds are given by the donor as endowment assets. For true endowment funds, the principal is permanently maintained with earnings available for expenditure. Quasi-endowment funds are designated by the church's governing body to function as endowment. These could come from surplus funds or if the church decides that all unrestricted bequests, or a portion of unrestricted bequests, will be designated as endowment funds. The principal from quasi-endowment funds may be used for other purposes by action of the governing body. Many church endowments contain a mixture of true and quasi-endowment funds.

Restricted and Unrestricted Endowment Funds

There are two types of true endowment funds. Restricted endowments are given for a particular purpose that determines how the earnings will be used. Unrestricted endowment earnings are available for use as determined by church policy or decisions. Churches do not have to accept a gift if the restriction does not fit their mission, if they are not capable of fulfilling the restriction, or if they simply do not wish to do so. But if a church accepts a restricted gift, it is bound to manage and use it in keeping with the donor's restrictions.

USING ENDOWMENTS TO BUILD THE FUTURE

Loren Mead said the "purpose of an endowment is to grow the church of tomorrow, not embalm the church of today."[1] This statement captures the positive potential of an endowment fund. An endowment should build a church's capacity to sustain and extend its mission in the future. Yet too often, endowments are used to preserve the status quo rather than serve the future.

Since the purpose of an endowment is future vitality and strength, the investment policies need to preserve the endowment's real value over the long term and the spending rate needs to be conservative enough that the principal grows at least enough to offset inflation. Churches maintain this future perspective by clearly stating the endowment's purpose, investment policy, spending policy, and how undesignated bequests are used.

Purpose

Churches have great latitude in using unrestricted endowment earnings so long as the spending aligns with the church's mission. Discerning the goals of the endowment will provide focus and help assure that the funds are used fruitfully. The development of a "so that" statement is a simple way to clarify your purpose: *We will establish an endowment so that . . . .* The rest of the sentence needs to describe the change you desire because of the endowment.

Here's an example of a weak "so that" statement. *We will establish an endowment so that we will have a fund for people who want to leave money for the church to carry out its ministry.* It is a poor statement because so long as you establish the fund—even if no one gives to it or no funds are generated—you will have succeeded 100 percent in accomplishing your "so that." A stronger statement might be: *We will establish an endowment so that our church will reach and serve more people, younger people, and more diverse people.* Another example is: *We will establish an endowment to provide for capital expenditures and investments to free other funds for programs and immediate needs.* Both put the emphasis on the future rather than the past or present.

Some purposes that fit well with a future orientation include funding capital renewal and replacement needs, reducing debt, supporting new ministry initiatives, funding missions and outreach, and supporting ministry with children and youth. What these things have in common is that the money is going for things with a life longer than one year or are making possible ministry aimed to the future. They also free up more current giving to support current ministries.

Using endowment earnings for operating expenses is not out of the question, but this use needs to be much narrower and more limited than is often the case. Some operating funds may come from restricted endowment. For example, endowment given for music ministry may provide some or the entire music portion of the budget.

MANAGING AN ENDOWMENT

Establishing an Endowment

An endowment must be established by a church's governing body in accordance with relevant legal requirements, denominational polity, and church bylaws. The governing board's resolution to create an endowment will normally establish the purpose of the endowment, uses of the funds, investment policies, spending policies, and dissolution procedures. The governing body then is responsible for electing directors for the endowment from candidates determined to be free of conflicts of interest. The endowment directors are always accountable to the governing board and the governing board's policies. Endowment directors should identify any congregational or denominational considerations regarding socially responsible investing.

Investment Policies

While this book does not offer investment advice, we can observe how churches seek both to preserve the value of the endowment and to provide income for ministries. There is a tendency to think it's best for churches to invest endowment funds in a way that guarantees the principal and to spend only the interest. But if you do this, the value of the fund will be declining each year by the rate of inflation. Even if the dollar amount of the principal remains the same, you can't do as much with that amount of money as when it was given. Your church should identify the rate of return needed to cover your spending rate and inflation over time. Normally this requires a mixture of equities and cash investments. Examine the percentage of stocks and bonds in your fund and get advice on how to balance your investments to allow enough total return growth (interest, dividends, and appreciation) to provide a reasonable spending rate for ministry each year (4 percent, for example) while also replacing the cost of inflation. This maintains the purchasing power of the endowment. Using your judicatory foundation to manage the funds can be of great help. They offer a range of funds depending on your goals and usually with low expenses.

Spending Policy

The practice of investing the principal and spending the earnings reduces the real value of your endowment every year by the rate of inflation. A sound investment policy requires prior attention to the spending policy. The goal is to set a spending rate low enough to allow a return to principal equal to inflation. Here's an example. Your spending rate is 4 percent and you assume an inflation rate of 2 percent. Therefore, you will need a total return over time of 6 percent. You need an investment policy that can reasonably achieve an average annual total return of at least 6 percent over any five- to eight-year period. Remember that total return includes interest, dividends, and appreciation. These figures and goals will change from time to time, particularly the assumed rate of inflation, so they need to be monitored regularly.

Establish a Bequest Policy

Even if your church has never received a bequest, it needs a bequest policy. If you receive an unanticipated bequest without having a policy in place, pressing needs or wants from various segments of the church will likely win out over using the bequest as endowment. Also, having a policy in place signals to those considering a gift of lifetime assets that you are prepared and a worthy recipient of their gifts. Your policy should make clear your commitment to honor the restrictions on any gift you choose to accept, but also leave the option of refusing a restricted gift that does not fit your mission, values, or capabilities. The policy should also specify how unrestricted bequests will be used. A future orientation will direct them for purposes with a longer horizon than immediate needs. Generally, churches put undesignated bequests toward the endowment, the capital fund, or divide them between these two funds.

PRACTICAL STRATEGIES FOR STARTING AND GROWING AN ENDOWMENT

Seek Guidance

If your denomination or judicatory has a foundation, your first step should be to learn what assistance they offer. Typically, a foundation can provide advice on establishing an endowment, assistance in developing a planned giving program, and investment services. Working with such a foundation is often particularly helpful for small congregations or congregations with relatively small endowments.

Create a Planned Giving Team

Churches typically do a poor job of encouraging gifts from lifetime assets. One reason for this failure is that no one attends to this need on an ongoing basis. Building an endowment is a classic example of something that is important but not urgent. Just as you need a team to give leadership to your annual stewardship campaign, you need a team focused on planned giving. The members of the team might be connected to your stewardship or finance committee or the group responsible for the management of your endowment, but giving some individuals on the team the single responsibility of focusing on planned giving will help assure that it doesn't get lost in the shuffle or always lose out to short-term financial planning considerations.

Educate Congregants about the Importance of Having a Will

One of the simplest things a congregation can do to help members properly steward their lifetime assets is to stress the importance of having a will. According to Gallup research, more than half of Americans do not have a will. Even among older and upper-income Americans, 30 percent of those sixty-five and older and almost 40 percent of those with incomes of $100,000 or more do not have a will.[2] The assets of those who die intestate (without a will) are distributed on the basis of state law.

Offering workshops on estate planning and wills is not only a good stewardship strategy, it is also good pastoral care because it helps people tend to the needs of their heirs. But even people who understand the importance of a will are prone to procrastinating. So put a small item in your church newsletter on a regular basis explaining why a will is an important aspect of personal financial stewardship. Then, keep up the drumbeat with simple reminders in the worship bulletin or newsletter. "Have you made a will?" "Is your will up to date?" "Have you considered remembering the church in your will?"

Encourage Proportionate Giving from Estates

Whenever you discuss tithing or proportionate giving, remember to mention that it doesn't only apply to current income. One of the simplest ways for someone to make an estate gift is to specify that a percentage of their estate go to the church. This is superior in many ways to specifying a gift of a set amount. Imagine two church members whose wills direct a $25,000 gift to the church. When they wrote their wills in 1982, that seemed like the perfect amount. But the overall value of one person's estate multiplied over the subsequent decades, so that the amount now represented a very, very small percentage of lifetime assets, even though it seemed quite generous in 1982. The other church member's assets had dwindled over the years due to health-care expenses, so that the $25,000 gift was so large it prevented the person from achieving other legacy goals. As these examples illustrate, it is better to encourage people to give a percentage of their estate, hopefully at least equal to the percentage of income they gave in their lifetime. Another way to think of tithing one's estate is to make lifetime gift that would provide ongoing income equivalent to the tithe paid during one's lifetime.

Form a Legacy Society

Churches and other charities often draw attention to the importance of estate giving by forming a group recognizing people who have the church in their wills. Creating such a group is a good way to start a conversation about planned giving. It encourages members to act on their intentions and celebrates the importance of making lasting gifts to the church. As a practical matter, people who are childless or whose children are grown are often the most open to considering a planned gift. An annual legacy society event is the perfect opportunity to reach out to these people and others.

Those born between 1946 and 1964 (baby boomers) are the richest generation in history. They currently control at least 70 percent of all disposable income.[3] And the estimated $30 trillion in assets they will distribute through their estates will be the largest ever generational transfer of wealth.[4] For the many congregations whose pews are full of older adults, this is a now-or-never moment. Helping this generation of church goers faithfully steward their lifetime assets will be critical to the future viability of many congregations. In the Proverbs it is written that "the good leave an inheritance to their children's children" (Proverbs 13:22). Planning for the future is part of responsible stewardship for both individuals and congregations.

Chapter 13

The Importance of Paying Attention

A church can exercise great care in conducting a pledge drive and constructing responsible budgets, but these efforts may add up to nothing more than good intentions if the church isn't paying attention to how giving and spending measure up to plans. Leaders help define and interpret reality, and nowhere is an accurate understanding of reality more important than in church finances. Because virtually every aspect of the church is touched by its financial health, pastors and other church leaders need systems for monitoring financial performance.

MONITOR GIVING MORE REALISTICALLY

Giving trends are one critical measure of a church's financial health. It is important to track giving as accurately as possible throughout the year. Nine out of ten churches use one method in reporting the status of their budget goals—they divide their annual budget by fifty-two then define what is "needed each week" as 1/52 of the annual budget. Alongside this amount they report the weekly receipts. From that they determine what is "needed to date" based on the number of weeks that have transpired, and then they compare this amount with their income to date and show a surplus or deficit.

Why This Common Practice Doesn't Work

This practice appears perfectly logical except for one fact. People do not give in such a pattern. Congregations do not receive money equally each week or month through the year. Therefore, people give according to one pattern, while churches monitor their giving based on another pattern. In some churches, the budget performance reported to members may show a "deficit" all year through November and then by the end of December the budget is raised. This is not because church members finally notice the deficit in December and give more. Rather, these churches always receive much more in December than at any other time of the year.

Your church has its own unique pattern of giving. And the standard method of reporting based on fifty-two equal shares of the budget does not provide an accurate reading of how well your church is doing financially as the year goes by. Most importantly, monitoring giving against equal weekly or monthly expectations does not answer the pressing question: "How likely is it our church will raise its budget in full by the end of the fiscal year?"

Discovering Your Unique Congregational Giving Profile

What is an alternative? An alternative is to monitor giving throughout the year based on the way people in your congregation tend to give. We call this unique pattern of giving your Congregational Giving Profile or CGP. The Lewis Center for Church Leadership offers a CGP resource (downloadable or DVD/CD set) with preset formulas for calculating your CGP.[1] However, it is also possible to create your own spreadsheets if someone has basic Excel knowledge.

The first step is to assemble a record of weekly giving during the past three years. Include all contributions toward the operating budget but not income from other sources, such as rental income, endowment, grants, and the like. You should also exclude any large onetime gifts. These data should be set up in columns so that you can see the average amount received each week over the most recent three years and the cumulative year-to-date income you typically receive through each week of the year. For example, over the past three years, the average giving in the first week was $4,000 and in the second week it was $3,500. This means that, on average, $7,500 was raised in the first two weeks, which is 3 percent of your $250,000 annual goal. That will be your benchmark for week two in the current year.

Record the average amounts and the running totals for each week to set goals for the whole year. If people ask the origin of these goals, you simply say they are based on when people in your congregation tend to give each year. The important figure to monitor is not so much how one week's giving compares to the weekly goal. Rather, each week after the first week you have a more reasonable year-to-date goal. You can easily see how much money you need to receive through the most recent week based on how people typically give in your church. Summer slumps and end-of-year surges are all factored in the calculations.

You Must Still Pay Attention

This system of reporting requires close attention to what giving figures reveal. Under the old system, it is easy to become accustomed to running deficits for much of the year, assuming the money—or at least most of it—will come in at the end of the year. This new system is a much more precise budget measure. For example, if after a few months using your CGP to monitor giving your church is consistently running about 10 percent behind in giving, it is reasonable to expect it will end the year with a 10 percent shortfall. If the projected deficit is large enough, the church may need to adjust spending plans to account for the shortfall. It is much better to discover such patterns in the early months than when most of the year has passed. On the other hand, if a church is running even or somewhat ahead of expectations based on CGP calculations as the year progresses, chances are very good that the year-end financial picture will be positive.

KEY MEASURES OF YOUR CHURCH'S FINANCIAL HEALTH

Many churches are used to thinking of finances one year at a time. And the measure of financial success is if the congregation "makes the budget" each year. Such a perspective often misses longer-term patterns and trends. Monitoring certain key indicators can help gauge your church's long-term financial health. The goal isn't to judge but to test out your current financial situation to see what needs attention and to begin a conversation with key leaders. Financial leaders should periodically determine the answers to the following questions.

What Percentage of Operating Revenue Is Recurring and Predictable?

Ideally, a church's ongoing operating expenses should be covered by recurring and predictable sources of income, such as pledges and offerings, program and facility fees, fundraisers, and the percentage of rental income not directed to support your capital budget. If your church relies too much on nonrecurring or unpredictable sources of income, such as receiving large onetime gifts or bequests, drawing from reserve funds, or spending too high a percentage of an endowment, then this is cause for concern. The operating budget income history chart in table 13.1 can help diagnose an unhealthy reliance on nonrecurring or unpredictable sources of income.

Table 13.1 Operating Budget Income History

	20XX	20XX	20XX
Recurring/predictable income			
Contributions and offerings	$	$	$
Building use income	$	$	$
Fundraisers	$	$	$
Endowment (4% spending rate)	$	$	$
Other recurring income	$	$	$
Total recurring income	$	$	$
Nonrecurring/unpredictable income			
Endowment drawdown (spending above 4%)	$	$	$
Bequests	$	$	$
Reserve or other funds to cover deficit	$	$	$
Other nonrecurring income	$	$	$
Total nonrecurring income	$	$	$
Grand total income	$	$	$
Recurring percentage of total income	%	%	%
Nonrecurring percentage of total income	%	%	%
Total	100%	100%	100%

How Are People Giving?

As we have seen, the trend away from using cash and checks for financial transactions has been constant and steep in recent decades. Churches have been slow to respond. Offering expanded options for giving to the church can be as freeing for members today as when churches allowed checks to be used for contributions. How many ways do you offer for people to contribute to your church? To what extent is your church's income limited by when and how members may contribute? Completing the ways people give chart illustrated in table 13.2 permits you to see your trends in utilizing expanded ways your members give. In addition to cash and checks received during worship services, what funds come through automatic withdrawals, mail, online giving, or other newer ways people handle their finances?

How Much Giving Comes from Persons Aged Seventy or Older?

Some churches have experienced an increase in giving even as average attendance has declined. Often a significant portion of this generous giving comes from older, loyal church members. Most of these donors did not start out giving at such levels. They usually advance to their current level of giving through a combination of growth in discipleship and increased financial resources. Generous givers of the future probably will follow the same route. Therefore, to neglect reaching new people and teaching stewardship

Table 13.2 Ways People Give

	20XX	20XX	20XX	20XX	20XX
Cash and checks given in worship offerings					
Other ways of giving					
Total	$0	$0	$0	$0	$0

	20XX	20XX	20XX	20XX	20XX
Cash and checks in worship offerings %	%	%	%	%	%
Other ways of giving %	%	%	%	%	%
Total	100%	100%	100%	100%	100%

because the church already "meets its budget" through the generosity of a few is shortsighted ministry. It is typical for middle-aged and older givers to be more generous to the church. But if the percentage of giving that comes from those aged seventy or older grows larger each year, it represents a point of vulnerability. So, it is important to know this statistic. Even if you do not know everyone's exact age, you can make an educated guess.

Is Any Expense Category Threatening Sustainability?

Has one component of your budget become so disproportionate that it jeopardizes the church's future? You will want to examine three things: (1) your debt, which is often a problem for newer churches; (2) your pastoral compensation, which can be overly burdensome for smaller congregations; and (3) your facility costs, particularly if your congregation has older, expansive facilities that no longer fit the size of the congregation. All these expenses are appropriate, but the danger comes if one requires such a large share of the church's resources that it compromises the ability to fund other important aspects of ministry. If short-term solutions no longer resolve the financial dilemma, some churches may need to question their long-held assumptions. Can the congregation still afford to maintain its current building? Should it consider a less than full-time pastor? Should merger be explored? These are difficult questions to raise. It is far better to begin these conversations when there are still options rather than waiting until there are fewer people, possibilities, and financial assets.

Are You Deferring Maintenance?

One common way for congregations to balance budgets in challenging times is to defer maintenance. Consider what should ideally be spent each year to fund at least a minimal level of ongoing capital renewal and replacement needs in categories such as safety, accessibility, heating and cooling, roofs, painting, technology upgrades, and renovations. If you are consistently budgeting less than is needed for capital renewal, you are risking greater expense down the road. And even if you can't fund everything right away, it's helpful to know the demands for the funds you do have.

Is Your Endowment or Permanent Fund Invested to Maintain Its Value?

As we have seen, there is a tendency to think it's best for churches to invest endowment funds in such a way that the principal is guaranteed and spend only the interest. Even if the dollar amount remains the same, you can't do as much with that amount of money as you could when it was given. Examine the percentage of stocks and bonds in your fund and get advice on how to balance your investments to allow enough total return growth in the fund so you can have a reasonable spending rate for ministry each year while also replacing the cost of inflation.

Is Your Spending Rate Appropriate?

If churches spend all the earnings from their endowment each year, their endowment value decreases each year by the rate of inflation. Many churches seek to return to the principal an amount equal to the rate of inflation by setting long-term investment goals that protect the value of the endowment while providing funds for ministry. To accomplish this, many use an asset allocation with between 40 and 60 percent of the endowment in equities. How is your endowment invested? What is your effective spending rate now? The recent endowment effective spending rate chart in table 13.3 permits you to see at what rate you have spent from your endowment in recent years. Is this sustainable? Does this rate reduce the real value of the endowment?

Table 13.3 Recent Endowment Effective Spending Rate

	20XX	20XX	20XX	20XX	20XX
Endowment market value previous June 30					
Withdrawals, expenditures, and expenses this year					
Effective spending rate (spending divided by market value)					

Asking these questions can give you fresh insight into your church's overall financial health. Regularly considering these issues and taking appropriate action can strengthen your financial practices and policies to ensure that the mission of your church thrives for years to come.

Chapter 14

Financial Oversight and Integrity

In writing to the church at Corinth, the Apostle Paul makes clear his intent to treat with great care the offering he is taking for the church in Jerusalem. Paul wants to do right not only in the Lord's sight but also in the sight of others. Even in these early days of the church, Paul was keenly aware of the need for maintaining what we today would call financial integrity. Paul knew that any perception of financial impropriety would damage his ability to proclaim the gospel effectively. The same is still true for the church today.

When persons contribute to our congregations, they are giving tithes and offerings to fulfill the church's mission. Church leaders have a solemn responsibility to keep their sacred trust to ensure that gifts are handled properly and used in judicious and faithful ways. Christian giving is an expression of stewardship that requires leaders of churches to be faithful stewards of those resources.

In some churches, particularly smaller churches, there may be a tendency to think everyone has the highest ethical ideals and best of intentions, so all the standard rules of handling money need not apply. In such situations, attempts to introduce financial integrity standards where they have been missing can be interpreted as judgment on individuals. Such is not the case. In fact, anyone involved with the church's money should insist that proper protocols are in place to protect themselves from temptation and the possible appearance of impropriety.

Every church needs financial policies detailing how it handles contributions. Such policies demonstrate that the church treats giving as an act of worship in response to God's great gifts. Such policies ensure that gifts are preserved and used to advance the church's mission. When people know their gifts are properly administered, they have greater confidence in their church and its leaders. Well-thought-out policies protect the giver by ensuring

117

the proper administration of the gift. And these policies also protect those volunteers and staff who handle gifts from accusations or perceptions of mismanagement. Lack of trust in church financial systems leads to lower giving.

GOVERNANCE AND LEADERSHIP

Congregational leaders must set the tone for how church finances are viewed and handled. The pastor must affirm, respect, and adhere to financial control policies. The finance committee and governing board must assume that proper procedures are in place and followed consistently. The leadership sets the tone. Church leaders need ongoing engagement in reviewing and guiding the finances of the church.

Governing Body

It is crucial for the governing body of the church to be involved actively in the financial oversight of the congregation. Board neglect almost always leads to ineffective, if not improper, use of funds. A well-informed and engaged governing body that holds together financial procedures and mission faithfulness leads to accountability and fruitfulness. This does not mean that the governance role of setting policy and oversight gets confused with management. The pastor, staff, and ministry leaders of the congregation must have the managerial responsibility to carry out the ministry within the church's policies and budget. Daily operational management is not the responsibility of the governing body.

One of the most essential functions of the governing body is to approve the annual budget upon recommendation of the finance committee and in accordance with denominational polity or congregational policies. Budgets can be changed during the year if conditions require it. The governing body receives detailed reports from the finance committee at each meeting. Expenditures not covered in the approved budget or through other established policies must be approved by the governing body. The governing body also receives the report of the annual audit.

Finance Committee

The finance committee submits the annual budget for approval by the governing body in accordance with established procedures. Monthly financial reports are prepared by the treasurer and are submitted to the finance committee for review. From the finance committee, the reports go to the governing body and to those who manage the budget. Any significant budget variances should be noted and explained. The finance committee is responsible for oversight and enforcement of all policies and practices. The finance committee initiates any changes in policy and to new policies in preparation for submission to the governing body for approval.

Pastor

The pastor, along with lay leadership, is responsible for setting a tone of financial integrity and ensuring that the church's financial policies are carried out. The pastor should lead in adhering to the policies and expect such adherence from others. The pastor also needs to display confidence in the finance committee and their procedures. The pastor also should review weekly and monthly financial reports and indicators and confer with finance leaders about trends and implications. The pastor should help finance leaders identify financial policies that need to be added or revised.

INTERNAL CONTROLS

The church has a responsibility to ensure that funds given to the church are used in a manner consistent with the church's mission and any donor restrictions. Internal controls—the policies and practices that govern the day-to-day receipt and disbursement of funds—help ensure secure and accurate handling and reporting. A key principle underlying internal controls is the *separation of duties*. Such separation of duties ensures that no one person has access to more than part of the receipt or disbursement processes. By separating duties, a church lessens the chances of simple errors and the opportunity for misappropriation of funds. Therefore, such roles as counting, recording, and reconciliation are separated in the receipts process. In the disbursement process, the roles of authorization, generation, signing, and reconciliation are separated. In a small church, it may be more difficult to obtain such clear separation of duties. But small churches can still separate some of the duties and consider rotating the roles on an annual basis. Internal controls are also important in preventing and detecting fraud and protecting the church's assets. Internal controls benefit not only the church but also the employees and volunteers of the church.

Procedures for Receiving Funds

There are several important things to consider regarding receipt of funds. First, when counting and depositing funds, multiple unrelated persons should be present and involved in handling funds that come in worship offerings.

Ideally the same persons are not counting every Sunday. Second, churches receive funds at times other than the Sunday offering. Be sure to develop procedures for how funds received during the week are handled. Third, many churches now receive funds electronically. Be sure you have procedures in place to count and record these gifts.

Procedures for Disbursing Funds

The primary way a church authorizes the disbursement of funds is through the budget approved by the governing body. There are other things to keep in mind regarding the disbursement of funds. First, any disbursement needs to be documented. Bills or receipts should accompany any request for disbursement. Second, consider having multiple signers for checks. Churches sometimes require two signatures on checks larger than a designated amount. Also keep in mind the need for multiple authorized check signers in case one signer is not available. This eliminates the need ever to sign blank checks. Third, be sure to secure blank checks under lock and key.

Monthly Reconciliation

Each month a person who has not been involved in either the receipt or disbursement processes should reconcile all bank statements. The results of this reconciliation should be reported to the treasurer and the finance committee. It is important to do this task each month so that problems can be identified quickly, and steps taken to prevent future problems.

Financial Audits

Of course, the cornerstone for a church's financial integrity plan is the annual financial audit. An audit builds confidence in the financial processes of the church, identifies potential risk areas, and offers suggestions for improvement. Most importantly, it protects both those who give and those who handle the gifts. An audit will verify that transactions have been handled properly and that proper internal controls and separation of duties are in place.

There are several options available to congregations. Some require a Certified Public Accountant (CPA) and some don't. They vary in cost. An *external audit* is conducted by a CPA. One denomination suggests that churches with income of $500,000 or more utilize a CPA. While costlier than other options, a church of any size may need an external audit, for example to comply with a mortgage agreement or for other reasons. An *internal review* is done by a church member or members who are not part of the financial handling processes of the congregation. This is cost effective for many smaller congregations. Many denominations provide guidelines and forms to conduct an internal audit.

An *audit exchange* enables a review by people familiar with financial matters and procedures from another congregation. This is cheaper than a traditional audit and may be free if you trade reviews with another congregations. If this is new for you, the first time will be the hardest. But get started and continue each year. The benefits far outweigh the time and effort.

Inventory of Assets, Insurance, and Bonding

Controls should be in place to protect property and equipment owned by the church. All such assets should be catalogued, insured, and accounted for on an annual basis. Keep all securities in a bank safe deposit box. Keep an inventory of the contents of the safe deposit box and at least once a year make sure the contents match the inventory.

Churches should conduct a periodic review of the church's insurance policies. Attention should be paid to making sure there is adequate coverage and that deductibles are acceptable. In addition, persons who handle church funds regularly should be bonded and churches should purchase directors' and officers' liability insurance to protect volunteers.

COMMUNICATION

Regular communication about church finances is an important step in building trust and establishing a culture of transparency. Not everyone in the church needs to know everything. The most detailed information will be shared with the pastor, finance committee, and governing board. In addition to these reports, it is important for the pastor and finance leadership to communicate appropriately with the congregation regarding the church's finances. These reports will be of overall trends and patterns rather than the detailed reports prepared for the finance committee.

Simple reports on church finances throughout the year remind members that those elected and hired to handle financial matters are doing their work and are accountable to the congregation. For example, upon completion of the annual audit, a simple printed announcement for the next few weeks that the audit is complete and available will send an important signal that someone is "taking care of business." Few will access the audit report, but all will feel better that the finances are being handled properly and that they have access to basic church financial information.

One important part of communications is regular reports of giving to contributors. This allows you to thank contributors, report on good things accomplished through their giving, and report on the state of church finances. Be sure to include with any statements the person to contact if there are errors in the report.

As you think about practices and policies for your church, be reasonable in what you propose and implement. And make sure the benefits of changes you introduce outweigh the costs of implementation. It is tempting to think that smaller churches do not need such policies. But because every church receives and disburses funds, every church, regardless of size, needs to safeguard its financial integrity as a way of advancing its mission. Jesus said, "Whoever is faithful in very little is faithful also in much" (Luke 16:10). Through prudent financial oversight churches demonstrate themselves to be worthy stewards of the treasure their members entrust to them.

Part III

ABUNDANCE

Chapter 15

God's Promise of Abundance

God's promise of abundance is the third core theological affirmation shaping our relationship with money and possessions. Our abundant God is all-sufficient and overflowing—a God who created a bounteous world and desires that all people experience the fullness of life in every possible way—physical, mental, spiritual, emotional, and material. This is why Jesus said, "I came so that they might have life, and have it abundantly" (John 10:10). Images of abundance abound in Scripture, from the beauty and simplicity of the Garden of Eden to the detailed depiction of the New Jerusalem. Abundance is the beginning and the end of salvation history. It is God's desire for all of creation.

On the surface, God's abundance may seem almost indistinguishable from God's generosity. This is because generosity, stewardship, and abundance are intricately interconnected in the economy of God. It can be helpful to think of abundance as the goal and generosity and stewardship as the means by which that end is achieved. However, the relationship among the three is not linear but rather circular. By virtue of God's generosity, God entrusts things to our care. When we steward those things wisely, we are able to participate in God's generosity and help bring forth God's abundance. Faith in God's abundance frees us to open our hands in generosity. And a bold embrace of our responsibilities as stewards moves us from timidly hoarding what God gives us to using it to propel abundance.

Too often, we confuse God's promise of abundant life with the cultural definition of "the good life." We mistakenly think it involves ever-increasing wealth and possessions. But the Christian notion of abundance means *God will provide for our needs—not satisfy our greed*. No story in the Bible makes this more evident than God providing manna, the bread from heaven, to the Israelites as they journeyed through the wilderness. God generously provided for their needs, sustaining them through forty years in the desert in a surprising and unexpected way. Manna could not be stored. When the sun grew hot, it melted. There was no point in hoarding it. The people had to learn to trust in God's providence and accept the gifts that God provided. "Those who gathered much had nothing over, and those who gathered little had no shortage. They gathered as much as each of them needed" (Exodus 16:18). God provides for our needs but does not satisfy our greed. Or as Paul proclaimed, "God will fully satisfy every need of yours according to his riches in glory in Christ Jesus" (Philippians 4:19).

To equate the abundance of God with the material excess and overconsumption our culture promotes is another manifestation of the false prosperity gospel. Joe Daniels and Christie Latona explain that "abundance thinking helps to put prosperity in a proper perspective. Prosperity literally means to 'help another along the way.' . . . Living with an abundance mindset says there's enough out here for everybody, and if we do it God's way, there's more than enough for everybody."[1]

A LOAVES AND FISHES MENTALITY

Recall our earlier discussion of the miracle of the loaves and fishes. The people gathered to hear Jesus were operating out of a mindset of scarcity. The disciples, too, had a mindset of scarcity. But once they were assured that Jesus would feed the crowd, everyone felt comfortable sharing their food. And suddenly there was more than enough for all. What appeared to be a situation of scarcity became one of abundance because people's attitudes had changed. They were changed by faith. This story shows that an attitude of scarcity can become a self-fulfilling prophecy but so too can an attitude of abundance.

Another story of abundance is the woman with the alabaster jar who anoints Jesus with costly ointment (Matthew 26:6–13). The disciples rebuke her for wastefulness saying the ointment could have been sold for a large sum and the money given to the poor. But Jesus praises the woman for her act of devotion. Her example of extravagant generosity is a counterpoint to our tendency to think too small and operate out of a paradigm of scarcity when God promises abundance.

Like the disciples, like the crowd on the Galilean hillside, we tend to embrace the paradigm of scarcity. The world's logic teaches us there is never enough. It says we must look out for our own interests by accumulating everything we can, like the rich fool in the parable who pulled down barns and build bigger ones when his land produced abundantly (Luke 12:13–21). Abundance requires that we step away from the mindset of scarcity. The greed, hoarding, and overconsumption that flow from a scarcity mindset undermine abundance. Generosity and sharing bring it forth.

Just as generosity and stewardship are profoundly countercultural beliefs, the doctrine of the abundance of God stands in sharp contrast to the dominant economic worldview. Our culture teaches us that there is never enough. Our faith teaches us that God has already given us everything we really need. Understanding the true nature of abundance allows us to temper our tendency toward greed and overconsumption.

A MINDSET OF ABUNDANCE

Churches, too, often see their circumstances through the lens of scarcity, failing to recognize assets and opportunities within their grasp. And the trap of scarcity thinking can propel a church downward. As resources dwindle a bit more every year, many declining churches wring their hands with worry but stand pat. Rather than using what God has entrusted to them to reach others and serve the world, they hoard it to preserve the trappings of church life they find comfortable. In the name of responsible stewardship, they trim and cut back more and more until they strangle the last bit of life out of their ministry and deplete all their resources. They imagine themselves to be prudent managers. But they are burying their talent in the ground and failing to reap an abundant harvest. ~~Here fourth panta~~

A mindset of abundance can reveal overlooked assets and open new possibilities. "Jesus taught his disciples and teaches us to assume that there's always a fish sandwich in the crowd," write Daniels and Latona. "There's always an unknown asset that can meet someone's need and resolve someone else's problem, that can connect people for a change and bring hope to people in despair. . . . An abundance mentality sees that all things are possible with God."[2] But as in the story of manna in the wilderness, God's abundance will likely manifest itself in a surprising, even extraordinary, way.

A mindset of abundance frees a church to think differently about its economic future and its mission. It invites congregations to explore a more holistic approach to economic sustainability that looks beyond the twelve-month horizon of an annual budget, to see revenue possibilities beyond tithes and offerings, to be more creative in deploying assets, to seek new partners and sources of support, and to embrace more efficient ways of sustaining their mission. Many new church plants and congregations serving the economically marginalized have long relied on more creative, entrepreneurial, and community-based ways of financing ministry. And increasingly, established congregations are looking to their example.

An abundant future for the church of the twenty-first century requires a new mindset and creative new approaches to economic sustainability. The contours of church life are changing so rapidly that in many settings a business-as-usual approach to church finances is insufficient to meet the challenges of the day. This does not mean we abandon the basics. In fact, we have to be even more diligent in carrying forward time-tested best practices. The church is still called to nurture generous disciples and manage its finances carefully. But at the same time, it must be nimble enough to think beyond the basics and embrace new possibilities. Abundance calls us to think outside the box.

Chapter 16

Recognizing the Value of Physical Assets

One emerging trend in church life involves a shift in how some congregations exist in relation to their buildings, property, and physical locations. Declining attendance is one reason. But it is not the only reason. Some churches, for example, built huge educational wings in the baby boom years that are now underutilized due to declining birthrates, changing family configurations, and less classroom-based approaches to Christian education. Others have large lecture halls used by adult classes in the post–World War II era that are often empty today. Even the most vital congregations typically have portions of their buildings that go unused part of the week. And for churches struggling just to get by, an overly large building can be a hindrance to mission and a drain on resources that hastens their demise.

More broadly, it seems that a less place-based approach to ministry may be taking shape in the twenty-first century. Increasingly, vital congregations go where people are rather than expecting people to come to them. This post-attractional reality has given rise to innovative ways of ministering to people in community settings, such as the Fresh Expressions movement.[1] The rise of digital ministry is another factor that may impact facility usage. The accelerating move to the Internet doesn't mean church buildings are unnecessary. But some foresee a future in which more congregations employ a hybrid model, similar to what has emerged already in the retail and educational sectors.

STEWARDING THE VALUE OF PHYSICAL ASSETS

Churches give great attention to how they spend their money to support their mission. Likewise, churches should consider their land and buildings as "shared assets"[2] of the community of faith to be used to the maximum for the mission. James Hudnut-Beumler suggests churches ask the question, "What are the best uses to which we can put this building (or camp, or bus), which we hold in common?"[3] The most obvious use of a church's property is for worship, education, fellowship, and community service. However, even active congregations have relatively low space usage compared to how other organizations use their space. So, exploring additional uses—whether to expand the church's ministry, support other groups, or generate revenue—is an exercise in prudent stewardship.

There is a saying that "farmers live poor and die rich" because many of a farmer's assets are tied up in land and equipment. This can pose economic challenges year to year for someone who, upon death, leaves an estate of enormous value. Churches are sometimes the same way—cash poor but property rich. They may have land, buildings, and no debt. These assets bring with them expenses of upkeep but little in the way of income. They are critical to the activities that express the church's mission. But it is important to ask how fruitful the assets are serving that mission, just as one would ask with any other investment.

David McAllister-Wilson, president of Wesley Theological Seminary, has observed that if the American church were a company its assets-to-income ratio would make it a prime takeover target. "We've got a lot of capital assets in the form of land that could produce a lot more revenue than it is now. We are overcapitalized. If we take our mission as seriously as 7-Eleven takes its bottom line, we need to see our property as a means to a greater end." For example, the net value of the assets of United Methodist churches is almost $63 billion. That comes to an average of over $2 million per congregation and over $25,000 per worshiper.

The American landscape is strewn with churches whose congregations have dutifully maintained their buildings, balanced their budgets, and perhaps even amassed endowments, but are failing to use these resources fruitfully to advance the gospel. Many declining congregations fall into the trap of trying to maintain their building as a monument to their faithfulness rather than seeing it as a resource in service of God's mission.[4] Mark DeYmaz, pastor of Mosaic Church in Arkansas, attributes this to an overly narrow understanding of stewardship, one that views good stewardship as simply maintaining buildings and preserving assets. While these are important aspects of good stewardship, DeYmaz says churches that merely maintain what they have are like the wicked, lazy steward in Jesus's parable who sat on his asset for fear of losing it.[5] Effective stewards are creative and entrepreneurial, investing what they have for the sake of mission, knowing that they are accountable for the fruitful use of what God has entrusted to them. "Whoever sows sparingly will also reap sparingly, and whoever sows bountifully will also reap bountifully" (2 Corinthians 9:6 ESV).

An abundance mindset invites us to see church buildings and property differently. We need to understand that they belong to God. Every acre, stone, floorboard, shingle, stained glass window, light fixture, and pew came into being through the generous giving of faithful members and must be used to advance the kingdom.[6] The critical question to ask is, "How can we use our buildings and property not only to serve God's purpose now, but to position our church for generations to come?"[7] For a church with eyes to see how their property could be used creatively, unused space can be a "goldmine of opportunity."[8]

The most typical way for most congregations, large and small, to capitalize on the value of their building is through rentals (discussed in depth in the next chapter). But other models include creative space-sharing arrangements with mission partners or community groups, redevelopment of buildings or land in partnership with commercial developers, and investment in mixed-use facilities that house church activities while also generating an income stream. While owning a building has long been a defining characteristic of a mature congregation, some congregations are rethinking how they live in relation to their physical space. Some are selling their buildings to focus resources on mission. Some house their staffs in coworking spaces to avoid investing in office overhead while others host coworking spaces for community members. While these approaches are still the exception to the rule, they may offer clues to financial sustainability for many more churches in coming years.

STORIES OF ABUNDANCE

Shawnee Park Christian Church in Shawnee, Kansas, grew quickly after its founding in 1978, building a sanctuary and education space on donated farmland. But it started to struggle in the early 2000s. After a season of prayer and discernment the congregation concluded that too great a share of its budget was going toward a large mortgage and keeping up an aging building. Motivated by a desire to devote more resources to hands-on mission, they decided to sell their property, relaunch as Shawnee Community Christian Church, and move to rented space in a commercial office park. The church now devotes 67 percent of its budget to real hands-on ministry, providing school supplies to local elementary school students and partnering with a food and clothing ministry in Kansas City. This demonstrable commitment to mission is now its primary calling card.[9]

Mosaic Church launched in 2001 with the mission of becoming a truly multiethnic church serving an economically disadvantaged community in Little Rock, Arkansas. In 2003, it leased a former Walmart that had been empty for eight years and set about the task of redeeming the space. Something

unexpected happened. During the eight-year period they occupied this building, crime went down by 12 percent within a mile radius of the church and
retail businesses started moving back into the formerly rundown strip mall.
When it came time to relocate again, Pastor Mark DeYmaz decided to capitalize on the lessons learned. The church purchased another abandoned big
box space, this time a Kmart. And this time, rather than having a landlord
benefit when new businesses were attracted to the area being revitalized by
the church, they became a "benevolent owner" leasing out retail space in a
way that blesses the community and provides a sustainable income stream to
fund the church's mission.[10]

Rev. Jacqueline Jones-Smith was appointed to Christ United Methodist
Church in St. Petersburg, Florida, in 2016. She was the first African American
pastor to serve this 128-year-old downtown church. In the once vital church,
about hundred people worshipped per Sunday in the 1,200-seat sanctuary.
The church could afford only a part-time pastor. It was rapidly exhausting
its endowment and facing possible closure. Jones-Smith was convinced this
strategically located church still had much to offer. But she also knew a turn-
around would require thinking outside the box.[11] She set about identifying
talent, assets, and opportunities and formed a business development taskforce
to assess options. In 2020, the congregation sold its parking lot to a developer
for $5.3 million with the promise of 120 free parking spaces on Sundays in
perpetuity.[12] The taskforce is now formulating plans to invest the money and
develop their remaining property to generate operating revenue and support
new ministry initiatives. "Business in not a bad word," says Jones-Smith.
"A business development focus is a vital element of pastoral ministry to support, maintain, and grow the church."[13]

Each of these churches faced unique circumstances shaped by their individual contexts, challenges, gifts, and callings. The way of claiming abundance was different for each. But these stories suggest that the leaders of any
church can take stock of its resources and think creatively about how they
might best be used to support its mission. For example, when Pastor Rosario
Picardo was starting a new church in an old building, he decided to inventory all of the church's assets. He came upon two old sets of silver handbells
that hadn't been used for twenty years. They were sold to another church for
almost $10,000 providing a much-needed infusion of cash to this fledgling
church plant.[14]

ASSESSING NEEDS AND POSSIBILITIES

A good first step is to assess your physical plant and current space usage in
the same manner described for capital budgeting in chapter 11. But ask a new

set of questions. Could classrooms that sit empty during the week be used for weekday childcare, adult learning classes, book clubs, music lessons, or exercise classes? Does your church have a commercial grade kitchen that might be rented to a local caterer or food truck operator? Would a portion of your property have value for a long-term lease to a business or a housing development? If your church is in a commercial area or urban setting, would businesses or individuals be interesting in renting parking on weekdays or overnight? Could your larger gathering spaces be made available for receptions or family and neighborhood gatherings? Are there spaces that community choirs or drama groups might use for rehearsals and performances?[15] (Interestingly, there are now a number of online booking services similar to Airbnb that facilitate short-term rentals for meetings, events, social gatherings, workspaces, etc.)

This will also require some consensus on what space uses are really essential to your congregation. What space-use patterns are driven by wants rather than needs? And how might space be used differently or more efficiently? Most of us know space only the way we have seen it used. An office is an office. A classroom is a classroom. This keeps us from seeing the richness of what we may already have. It's a good idea to find those who can see your space more objectively and are capable of envisioning how it might be repurposed to meet your needs. An excellent book to help you steward your property in this way is *The More-with-Less Church: Maximize Your Money, Space, Time, and People to Multiply Ministry Impact.*[16]

Finally, it is important to consider what's going on around you. What are the unmet needs or unrealized opportunities in your community? How might your church bless the community while also leveraging the value of underutilized assets? Look for those who can help you explore options and learn from other churches in your area. The Wesley Community Development Corporation in North Carolina is one group that helps churches think through such issues. It is a nonprofit that helps churches develop or repurpose real estate to meet church and community needs. Another is Partners for Sacred Spaces, headquartered in Philadelphia, that works with congregations across the country to reimagine how their space might be used creatively in partnership with community organizations.

THE CHURCH IS NOT A BUILDING

Helping a congregation see its building as a resource for mission can be a challenge. From childhood, people are taught to associate the word church with a building and even taught to think of it as "God's house." And they understandably feel deep affection for the place where they have celebrated critical life passages.[17] Moreover, there are people present in your church who have sacrificed and labored over years, even generations, to acquire, build, or maintain their church building. Sometimes this investment leads to an "antiquated sense of ownership that allows longtime members to forget that the church building belongs to God, not to the members themselves, no matter how hard they have worked to maintain it."[18]

Such a mindset shift requires a compelling vision, persistent leadership, and theological clarity. Pastor Audrey Warren led First United Methodist Church of Miami through the process of selling its church, prominently located on Biscayne Boulevard, to a commercial developer. The first step was helping the congregation look objectively at its financial future. "The congregation needed to reduce its budget by $30,000 a year if something didn't change," said Warren. "The data told the story. And once the facts were on the table, people could see the reality." But it was also a matter of reminding the church why its presence in the community mattered. With tens of thousands of people moving into downtown Miami, the church saw a tremendous missional opportunity. Rather than using the significant proceeds of the sale to relocate, they struck a deal with the developer. New space for the church will be located at its old address, on the lower floors of a fifty-story apartment tower designed to be affordable and attractive to the young professionals moving into the neighborhood. "Our church is still committed to wanting Jesus to be known in downtown Miami," says Warren. Their new space will put them under the same roof as the new neighbors they seek to reach. "It was a matter of recapturing the missional imagination of a congregation that had a long history of risk-taking mission. It was a matter of putting purpose over preference."

Deploying building assets more strategically can generate income and contribute to a congregation's economic sustainability. But for Shawnee Community Church, Mosaic Church, Christ UMC, and First Miami it was more than just a matter of dollars and cents. The strategies they pursued also generated new mission possibilities and made the congregations more permeable and present to their communities. Abundance is unleashed when the stewardship of our resources is aimed at serving God's purposes, not a shadow mission of preserving a building or a particular way of worship.

Chapter 17

Best Practices When Renting Your Space to Others

In 2019, 62 percent of congregations received revenue from renting their facilities.[1] And rental income is likely to increase as more churches seek to diversify their income and better use their physical assets. Yet many churches have a mixed mind regarding the use of their facilities for purposes beyond those of their congregation. Some churches have in their stories a time when a public school or another congregation met in their church building after a fire or during renovation. In other congregations, parishioners would be surprised by the number of "outside" groups that regularly or occasionally use church space. Most of these uses come about through random requests or members who are connected to service organizations, civic groups, and other secular endeavors. So, the issue is not whether church space is used beyond church activities. It is how to think about this space use from the perspective of stewarding the commonwealth of the congregation, remembering that all church assets come from money given for one purpose, to fulfill the church's mission.

WHY RENT YOUR FACILITIES?

James Hudnut-Beumler says that churches commonly make a number of mistakes in thinking about renting their facilities. Often the first mistake is to begin the conversation by asking how much to charge. But this misstep flows from a more fundamental mistake—failing to consider potential building use from the perspective of the church's mission.[2] This is really the only touchstone that matters.

The Lewis Center for Church Leadership works with a wide range of congregations across regional, denominational, racial, and size differences. We asked those that rent their facilities why they did it. The reasons overwhelmingly related to their mission—to serve their community, expand the church's outreach or community visibility, and attract new members. However, for at least a quarter of the churches the income was essential or at least very helpful to the congregation. While these responses are not necessarily representative of all churches, they do indicate a range of reasons for renting facilities. There may be other factors, but these responses show how they frame their practice publicly.

Whatever your motivation for renting facilities, Gerald W. Keucher reminds us to test out your assumptions before beginning or continuing a rental program. For example, if expanding the church's outreach or visibility is the goal, how would you assess if that is happening? If you hope to attract new members, how many have joined for this reason? Ask other churches about their experience. If the goal is to make money for the mission, then how much are you making after factoring in all costs?[3]

HOW MUCH SHOULD WE CHARGE?

While not the first question to ask, the matter of pricing rental space requires careful and nuanced thinking. Another common mistake churches make, says Hudnut-Beumler, is setting rental rates without considering the true costs associated with using the space. Often rental rates are set based on the first tenant or by other factors having little to do with either the nature of the use or the cost of providing the space. The answer to the question "How much rent should we charge?" depends on many variables and values. To make an informed decision, a church must first objectively consider how best to calculate the costs associated with the rental and then how to set the appropriate fee.[4]

Different Ways of Calculating Costs

It's important for everyone in the decision-making process to understand that there are several different ways to calculate the costs associated with renting space. No one measure settles your pricing structure. But understanding the different methods of calculating costs provides a more objective decision-making framework.

Average Cost

The average cost is calculated by adding up all facility costs (utilities, staff, repairs, insurance, maintenance, supplies, and capital reserve) for your whole building or physical plant and dividing that sum by the total number of square feet in the facility. This gives you the average cost per square foot per year. You can then calculate the average cost associated with a particular room or area based on its square footage. For example, if a daycare center is interested in exclusive use of a set of classrooms that comprise 20 percent of your church's total square footage, the average cost of that space would be 20 percent of your total facility costs. This may seem like a lot of work but once you know the square footage of your building and the spaces within it, the calculation is fairly easy and easily updated.

Marginal Cost

Calculating the marginal cost associated with a particular use of space assumes the church is paying the baseline costs of the space anyway, but additional or marginal costs will be incurred as a result of a rental. Such marginal costs might include additional utility, staff, or supply expenses related to preparing or cleaning the space or making it available beyond normal hours. For example, if a community choir wants to hold auditions in your sanctuary on a Saturday, you would calculate the incremental cost of having the custodian open the building and clean up afterward, having the lights on and the air conditioning running on a day they would normally be off, and setting up and operating the sound system. Again, calculating this on a onetime basis might seem like a lot of work, but you can quickly establish some benchmarks for the incremental cost of staff, utilities, supplies, and so forth.

Market Cost

A market cost calculation is based on the going rate for renting comparable spaces in your surrounding community. For example, if a small nonprofit wants to rent a three-room office suite in your building, you may want to know what comparable office space in your community costs. The challenge is often determining what is "comparable."

Opportunity Cost

Estimating the opportunity cost is not so much a financial calculation as a ministry judgment. How you use your facilities always brings trade-offs. You want to make sure the trade-offs are acceptable to your mission. For example, if you rent a portion of your parking lot on weekdays, what is the impact on church events scheduled during the week? Some trade-offs may turn out to be negligible. Others may be deal breakers.

Options for Charging

Just as you can view the cost of your facilities in different ways, you also have a variety of options for how you might set the rental fee in light of what you learn about costs.

No Charge

Charging nothing is always an option. Churches provide free space to congregational groups and various ministry activities, of course. But why treat an outside group the same? Generally, it's because the group's work is clearly aligned with the church's mission, the group offers a service the church is unable to provide, or the church sees a benefit in being associated with the group's values. For example, a nonprofit healthcare provider might need a place to serve low-income residents of the community and this supports the congregation's mission of serving the marginalized. The no-charge option needs to make sense in terms of your church's mission.

An In-Kind Contribution in Lieu of a Monetary Charge

This is similar to the no-charge option, but the group provides a gift or service in place of a monetary payment. An example might be a nonprofit offering a music program for children that started when similar programs were eliminated from the local public schools. Their gift in kind might be sharing music in worship or for congregational events throughout the year.

Marginal Cost

This involves charging an amount based on the marginal cost calculations explained previously. This can be appropriate for the type of group you might not charge at all if they have regular funding. For example, the healthcare nonprofit might have a government or foundation grant. Their funders probably understand the need for space and are prepared to cover some rental expense. By charging the marginal cost, the church receives some rental income but also supports the goals of the program.

Between Marginal and Average Cost

In some situations, a rent based on marginal cost might seem too low, but one based on average cost seems too high. You always have the option of splitting the difference. This provides flexibility but keeps the rental rate within parameters informed by actual cost calculations.

Average Cost or Market Cost

There are times where charging market rates or near market rates is fitting, particularly when renting to for-profit enterprises. For example, a nearby business wants to rent some of your parking during the workweek or a catering business occasionally needs additional kitchen space. In such cases, rates could be based on rentals in similar commercial settings.

OTHER CONSIDERATIONS

Any time a church rents space, even on a onetime basis, having a written agreement is in the interest of both parties. This is true even if the space is provided at no cost. The agreement can be simple and based on a standard template. Searching online for church rental agreements or sample leases will provide a sense of what categories to cover. It's important, for example, to clarify the responsibilities of both parties. Is the renting group or the church responsible for setting up and taking down tables and chairs? Opening and closing the building? Running audiovisual equipment or microphones? Are there certain times of year when the space will not be available? If so, spell that out. And always set an expiration or renewal date as a safeguard for all. Your aim is an agreement that an outside observer would deem fair to both parties.

Other key issues to consider before embarking on a rental program include the following: (1) the implications of rentals or other building use arrangement for your insurance coverage and liability; (2) the tax implications of rental income;[5] (3) any zoning restrictions or permit requirements; (4) any need for approval from your church's governing bodies or denominational authorities; (5) whether your child protection policies are applicable to building users; and (6) the advisability of a "hold harmless clause" in any agreement.

A BUILDING FULL OF PEOPLE

A well-thought-out rental strategy can produce income for a church. It can be a blessing to community groups and organizations needing space for worthwhile activities and services. It can forge new partnerships and extend the church's mission. And it can make your people, places, and programs more visible to community members as they come and go.

But some churches, particularly those whose internal programs are in steep decline, mistakenly believe that they have revitalized their church if they fill the building with other activities. Without a clear sense of how building uses align with their mission, such churches can become *de facto* community centers. A community center may be a very good thing, but it isn't the same thing as being a church. Rentals should always serve the church's mission either by supporting work that extends the church's mission or through arms-length financial transactions that generate revenue to support the congregation's core ministries. Rentals that serve these purposes can be instruments of abundance.

Chapter 18

New Partners and New Possibilities

Abundance invites a congregation to think differently about how its mission can be carried forward. Just as some congregations are rethinking the use of their physical assets, others are embracing new ministry models that attract new resources, engage new partners, or sustain the congregation's core ministries in less costly ways. And some find themselves at the point where they can no longer serve their mission. For them, the faithful question is whether church resources could be used more fruitfully to support other expressions of ministry.

GRANTS AND NONPROFITS

One potential approach to achieving abundance is drawing resources from beyond your congregation in support of your mission. The Rev. Sidney Williams calls this learning to "fish differently" by taking full advantage of all available resources, not just the contributions of members but also human resources, community partnerships, and creative financing possibilities.[1] Grants generally are not available to support a congregation's core, internal ministries beyond a limited pocket of funds from denominations, parachurch organizations, and a handful of religiously focused private foundations. But the interests of public and private funders can overlap with a congregation's mission, particularly in the realm of community outreach and social service programs.

Some churches organize themselves to take advantage of outside funding, generally by creating a separate section 501(c)(3) nonprofit legally distinct from the church to administer programs and receive grants. This approach enables the support of grantors and government agencies prohibited from supporting or reluctant to support religious causes. Many congregations expand their service and outreach and magnify their community impact through this strategy. Mosaic Church, for example, created an umbrella section 501(c)(3) called Vine and Village that stands alongside the church to operate community outreach ministries serving families, children, and youth.

"Grants can be a great resource. But congregations shouldn't think of grants as the cure to their money troubles," says Joy Skjegstad, an expert on community ministry and grant funding. "Churches need to consider what aspect of their ministry might be appropriate for outside funding, and what compromises they might have to make to take advantage of the money."[2] Creating a separate section 501(c)(3) probably isn't the right funding strategy for the average congregation. In addition to the legal steps required to set up a separate nonprofit organization, human and financial resources are required to operate the nonprofit and solicit outside funding. But congregations with sizable commitments to outreach ministries—community revitalization, child development, affordable housing, homeless services, feeding ministries, and so forth—should consider whether this approach might extend their reach and enhance their fruitfulness.

Emory Fellowship in Washington, DC, is one such church. This once run-down church in a historically African American neighborhood turned itself around by turning itself inside out. In 1996 it established Emory Beacon of Light, Inc., a nonprofit community development organization, to support work with the homeless and affordable housing. This led to a God-sized vision of constructing new affordable housing on their church property. This required partnerships with city and federal agencies, private funders, and real estate developers in both the commercial and nonprofit sectors. It took twenty years to develop the power, support, and resources to bring the dream to fruition. But in 2019, they cut the ribbon on the Beacon Center, a 180,000-square-foot campus that literally surrounds their historic church building and includes ninety-nine units of affordable housing as well as space for health and immigration services, youth programs, and new small businesses.

COMMUNITY PARTNERSHIPS

Sidney Williams says that drawing new forms of social capital in support of a church's mission begins with a very simple question, "With whom should we do ministry?" Established congregations are used to looking only within themselves for resources, overlooking the possibility that there may be social, political, or community groups that share their passions. In 2011, Williams was serving Bethel AME Church in Morristown, NJ, when Hurricane Irene hit. The church was flooded with four feet of water. Their flood insurance had lapsed. They had no savings. And they faced repair bills of over a $1 million. But drawing on a network of relationships among institutions and people who lived and worked in the surrounding community, the church was able to secure the funds to restore the church and launch a soup kitchen.[3]

In the basement kitchen of the St. Matthews Church fellowship hall in Morganton, North Carolina, there are two convection ovens, two gas ovens, a six-burner stove top, and a flattop grill. Sometimes there are twenty-four loaves of sourdough bread baking in one oven, and ten pies baking in another. From 7 a.m. until 11 p.m. nearly every day, church members bake, wrap, and label food. Since 2009, members have run Open Hearts Bakery, a full-scale operation certified by the North Carolina Department of Agriculture. Open Hearts is run by volunteers and all the money goes to church outreach projects. The work schedule frequently lists more than forty names from a church that averages about 100 in worship.[4]

While some community partnerships bring financial resources to support a church's work, more typically they fuel abundance by allowing a church to do more with less. Many churches take on new ministries without first taking stock of the good work that may already be going on around them. They end up reinventing the wheel, often creating programs that are costly or burdensome to maintain. Rosario Picardo says congregations can multiply the impact of their outreach by seeking out the people and organizations in their community already doing God's work and forging creative partnerships. He says "the financial reality is that churches alone can't possibly meet all the needs in our communities. But hundreds of people in our towns and cities are already doing God's Kingdom work daily!"[5] A church interested in helping children excel might think of launching an afterschool literacy program. Such a program could easily become a major undertaking with expenses for supplies, snacks, cleaning, and possibly additional staff. But the church might be able to achieve the same objective with far less cost and administrative overhead by connecting church volunteers with an existing tutoring program organized through the local public school.

CLAIMING ABUNDANCE IN THE FACE OF SCARCITY

Unfortunately, not every congregation can improve its financial circumstances or sustain its mission in these ways. Many face the unavoidable task of coming to grips with changed financial circumstances. When confronting harsh financial realities, the first instinct is to panic and then to assign blame. It is better to ask how to steward most faithfully the congregation's limited resources. It is important to consider the congregation's ministry in a larger context and apply the lens of mission.

Many congregations today find themselves in decline not because they have failed to minister faithfully, but because of larger demographic trends. In the United States, many of the church traditions that flourished in the twentieth century had grown rapidly in the nineteenth century and the early decades of the twentieth century. This was a time when the country was primarily rural, sometimes with 75 or 80 percent of the population living in rural areas. This is one reason these denominations have so many more congregations than those organized in later years as the population became more concentrated. Many of these churches remain where they were originally located while the population has grown more suburban and urban. The latest census showed that only 19 percent of the U.S. population lived in rural areas.[6] Furthermore, older persons are disproportionately found in rural areas.[7]

Not only has the population shifted away from the location of many congregations, so have jobs, schools, and other community institutions. The presence of churches in these communities is perhaps more critical than ever. But the combination of fewer people and older facilities often presents these churches with undeniable financial challenges. Some react with panic. Others deny these new realities until it is too late. This is especially the case if churches have some accumulated funds, which is often the case with smaller congregations.[8] They draw from those nonrecurring sources until the funds virtually run dry. When forced to address their situation more realistically, they discover there are few options because of the delay. Their accumulated assets have dwindled and are no longer available for capital or transition plans.

Is It Time to Consider a Part-Time Pastor?

A congregation may get to the point where the cost of a full-time pastor consumes such a significant portion of available resources that it is no longer sustainable. The idea of having a less-than-full-time pastor may seem like a drastic option. However, from biblical times until now, leadership in faith communities was often exercised by those who had other employment or responsibilities. The concept of one full-time pastor for one congregation is a relatively modern concept, though one that became the norm for many religious traditions. Many of the circumstances that made the full-time pastor normative (people, money, and available clergy) are not always present in churches today.

Another characteristic from older days that is coming back is the active involvement of a range of people in accomplishing the mission of a congregation. This is seen in vital larger and smaller churches. There are more part-time staff of all sorts serving congregations as well as growing numbers of non-paid persons who are assuming important ministry responsibilities. As one person at an Episcopal church that had moved to part-time clergy put it, "We are a community of practitioners, not consumers."[9]

There are two types of congregations with part-time clergy. One is a single congregation for whom their pastor serves part-time with other responsibilities outside the congregation. These other duties might include another profession or job, retirement, caring for family, or volunteer commitments. Another model is where two or more churches share the same pastor. The use of each model varies considerably by denominational history and culture. Congregations serving people of color and immigrants have routinely made use of the part-time model. Among mainline Protestant denominations, even where part-time pastoral service is practiced, there is often a sense that it is "less than" the ideal of a solo pastor. G. Jeffrey MacDonald has demonstrated in *Part-Time Is Plenty: Thriving without Full-Time Clergy*[10] the prevalence and rapid growth of part-time ministry among mainline traditions today.

STEWARDING YOUR LEGACY

Most congregations in the United States are small. Over 40 percent of congregations in the United States report average weekly attendance of fifty or fewer persons. And fully two-thirds of congregations have attendance of 100 or fewer. While most worshipers are found in larger churches, the reality of congregational life for most churches is functioning with a relatively small constituency base.[11]

A change to their staffing model may allow some of these congregations to continue fruitful ministry. But the same issues leading some churches to consider part-time pastoral leadership can in other churches prompt the question of whether the ministry should be discontinued. Just as human beings have a predictable lifecycle that ends in death, churches also have lifecycles. Many churches do not last through the startup phase. Others may endure for centuries. But all have a time of birth and a time of death.

We have already discussed how part of responsible stewardship for individual Christians includes considering what happens to our assets when our life comes to an end. If we plan carefully, our lifetime assets can help sustain our families and the legacy of our faith. But this legacy can be squandered if we do not plan appropriately. The same is true for congregations at the end of their lifecycle. They can squander the commonwealth of their congregation through inaction or they can consider how to leave a legacy that carries forward their mission.

The key question for churches is really the same in times of plenty and times of want. It is, "How do we best use the assets God has given us to accomplish our stated mission?" Even the smallest and most struggling churches have assets. And sometimes they have more assets per worshiper than newer congregations. There comes a time when every struggling congregation must ask, "Is the most faithful use of these assets to operate in the same manner until they all have been expended?" and "Could our remaining resources be instruments of love, compassion, and outreach for those whose names we may never know?" Some use the term "legacy church" to refer to congregations that discontinue their own ministry to sustain their broader mission in other ways. This term alludes to the overarching question: "What will the legacy of your church be?" The legacy of a church's mission is something to be stewarded.

Pastor Lee Ann Pomrenke shepherded a small Lutheran church through the painful process of bringing its ministry to a close. Instead of seeing this as a failure, she believes closing a congregation can be an act of faithfulness and responsible stewardship that can open the way to new life.[12] This new life coming from what appears to be death may take many forms. It could involve merger with another church. It could involve discontinuing the church's present ministry to allow a new congregation to take root in the space, or perhaps in a different place. Or, it may mean closing in a way that uses remaining assets to support new churches or other ministries and institutions that exemplify the church's mission. Our faith teaches us that death is not the end but the occasion for new birth. "We are resurrection people," writes Pomrenke, "but resurrection comes only after death. . . . Closing is not an indication that God has abandoned us or that we have abandoned God. Scripture bears witness to this, certainly, but so does our experience. When we are most bereaved, troubled, or feeling like failures, the Holy Spirit opens us to new possibilities."[13]

God showered abundance on the Israelites in the desert in the form of manna. It was not what they expected. Nor was it their preferred form of sustenance. But it was God's way of leading them toward a new future. In the same way, true abundance will not always conform to our preferences or established patterns. The faithfulness of our stewardship ultimately is measured by our willingness to adhere to God's purposes and relentlessly pursue God's mission. Jesus taught that new wineskins are needed to store new wine. Abundance sometimes requires that we stretch our missional imaginations and think outside the box.

CLOSING

Chapter 19

Developing a Comprehensive Year-Round Stewardship Program

Many church leaders complain that their congregations just don't seem to get it when it comes to giving and stewardship. And yet these leaders never talk about stewardship outside of a commitment campaign conducted in a perfunctory way over a couple of weeks culminating in the one and only stewardship sermon of the year. Creating a culture of generosity can't be done in a single Sunday or even in a month of Sundays. It's something that needs to be done on an ongoing basis throughout the year. Moreover, maintaining a solid system of financial management requires ongoing attention to a myriad of details that can easily fall through the cracks in busy churches.

Developing a stewardship calendar or planning template can help structure a more comprehensive and holistic approach to stewardship ministry. It can assure that all aspects of giving and financial management receive adequate and timely attention. It can keep the work of your stewardship and finance leaders on track. It can encourage consistent communication while avoiding overlapping appeals or messages. And it can reinforce a more holistic, theologically grounded sense of stewardship by connecting stewardship activities to scriptural and liturgical themes.

BUILDING A PLANNING TEMPLATE

The first step is to list the various aspects of stewardship and finance ministry that need to be put before the congregation regularly and then place them on a simple twelve-month timeline. Ask "what needs to happen?" and "when should it happen?" The goal is to make sure everything receives adequate attention without creating confusion. Consider the following categories.

Commitment Campaign

If your church conducts an annual stewardship or pledge campaign, block it out first on your timeline because it will influence the timing of other things. Many churches conduct their campaigns in the fall. This takes advantage of Thanksgiving as time to focus on gratitude and generosity, and it dovetails well with a budget year and pledge period that begin with the new year. But some churches find the beginning of the year a more logical and perhaps less crowded time to focus on commitment. And still others conduct their commitment drives in the spring, knowing that Easter is one of the most joyous and well-attended seasons of the church year. If your campaign culminates in a Commitment Sunday or other worship celebration, make that your anchor point. Add to your calendar any sermon series, special events, gatherings, mailings, and the like, and allow plenty of time for planning and follow up.

Stewardship of Time and Talents

In many churches, the annual stewardship campaign includes the opportunity for people to commit their time and talents to the church. The main benefit of this combined approach is that it projects a more holistic understanding of stewardship, communicating that it's not "all about money." In practice, though, time and talents often get short shrift in a combined campaign because of the urgency of securing financial pledges. So, some churches will focus on time and talents separately, generally before the financial campaign.

Budgeting

Creating an operating budget is a predictable annual exercise. Working backward from when the budget takes effect, plot out the necessary work and approval steps. Depending on the model used for creating the budget, this work can involve many different leaders and teams, so it's important to start early enough. Some churches that solicit pledges wait until the pledge total is known to finalize the budget. Others prepare the budget in advance of their commitment campaigns. For churches that budget on a calendar-year basis, much of this work will come in the fourth quarter of the year.

Fundraisers

Are some annual fund-raising events so much a part of your church culture that you couldn't stop them if you tried? An apple butter festival, rummage sale, homecoming, youth auction, or spaghetti dinner? If so, place them on your calendar. Such events tend to absorb a great deal of time and attention.

Putting them on the calendar will help you gauge whether too many fundraisers may be undercutting other ways of supporting the church's mission.

Vacation Periods

A summer giving slump is a fact of life in many churches. Late spring and early summer are good times to remind people to stay current with their giving or to set up a recurring online gift. The pastor of one prominent Texas church always preached his most potent message about generosity not on Stewardship Sunday in the fall but in June when people embark on their summer travels.

Special Appeals

Special giving opportunities can be an important part of a well-balanced stewardship program because they highlight key aspects of your mission and create on-ramps for new givers. Schedule these appeals to avoid donor fatigue or competing with messages about the importance of more regular giving. The less busy summer months can be a good time to schedule special mission appeals, especially if your church sends out mission teams or does other mission work over the summer.

Year-End Appeals

There's a reason why you receive so many charitable appeals in December. Many people do the bulk of their giving near the end of the year. Some want to generate tax deductions before December 31. Some may receive a portion of their compensation in the form of a year-end bonus. Many people feel particularly generous around the holidays. A few may even be motivated by the desire to see the church end the year in the black. So, consider adding a year-end appeal to your timeline in December.

Giving Statements

All churches should send out in January a record of contributions in the prior year for Internal Revenue Service (IRS) purposes. But many churches mail giving statements more frequently as a reminder to those who have fallen behind in their giving. Some send statements quarterly. But others send statements when they think they will have the most impact, for example, just before Easter and at the beginning of Advent. These are times when less regular attenders are more likely to attend services and catch up with their giving. So are late summer and early fall as congregants return from vacations. Regardless

of when you send statements, always include a thank you letter and information on how gifts are used in support of the church's mission. This makes the
statement less like a bill. And the money spent on postage does double duty.
No matter how you schedule your pledge reports, be sure that the last one goes
out in December as soon as all giving through November has been recorded.

Financial Reporting

Regular communication about church finances is an important step in building trust and establishing a culture of transparency. To remind the congregation that their gifts are well managed, include in the church calendar the dates
when reports are prepared and other financial tasks are handled. Stewardship
leaders should coordinate their work with finance leaders so that each supports the other. Some congregations receive regular updates on the church's
financial condition throughout the year. The language used for such updates
should always be consistent with stewardship theology and values. The last
thing you need is for your stewardship message to be that of a "Serve God's
Vision" church while the finance committee's message is that of a "Pay
the Bills" church.[1] Statistics about giving should always correspond to the
church's giving pattern that will vary predictably during the year. Statistics
that correspond to a static weekly or monthly benchmark give an unrealistic
impression of giving. Never miss the opportunity to include notices when the
annual church audit is complete and always indicate how people can see a
copy if they wish to do so. We know from experience that almost no one will
ask to see the audit, but the very notice itself, especially if done every year,
will build great confidence in the church's financial integrity.

Gratitude

Out of necessity, many churches are quite persistent in asking for money.
But they generally overlook two other interrelated forms of communication.
Asking should be part of an ongoing cycle of communication that connects
asking to both thanking people and telling the story of what someone's giving
accomplishes.[2] An effective ask always begins by thanking someone for what
they have already done. An effective thank you tells the story of what someone's involvement or contribution has made possible. And this telling creates
a positive climate for another ask. Ask! Thank! Tell! A comprehensive stewardship program should include a strategy for regularly thanking contributors
at key junctures—when someone makes a first-time gift or submits a pledge
but also along the way. Many leaders set aside time, weekly or monthly, to
thank donors by sending off a few handwritten thank you notes or making a
few phone calls. Some churches conduct an annual thank-a-thon or host an
appreciation event that is not an occasion to ask for pledges or contributions.

Planned Giving

A stewardship calendar can help assure that estate giving and other forms of planned giving aren't overlooked because of the continuing and sometimes urgent need to fund the operating budget. Some churches will schedule an annual Legacy Sunday to honor those who include the church in their wills and to invite others to do so. Memorial Day Weekend or All Saints Sunday can be logical times for this. Scheduling workshops on estate planning or other end-of-life planning might be another element of your timeline.

Financial Literacy Training

Education aimed at helping members better steward their own financial resources occurs on an ongoing basis in some churches. In others, it happens occasionally or not at all. Since getting on top of financial concerns is one of the most common New Year's resolutions (just behind diet and exercise), some churches focus on this early in the year. Other churches find ways to introduce stewardship education into the curriculum of ongoing groups or Sunday School classes.

A HOLISTIC APPROACH

Plotting out these key elements of stewardship ministry is more than a way to stay on top of the mechanics. It lays the groundwork for the more important work of weaving stewardship themes and activities into the warp and weft of congregational life. Once you've charted your yearly activities, you can focus on integrating them into preaching, teaching, and ongoing communication. Some wonderful tools can be found online suggesting ways that stewardship themes can be linked with congregational life and scriptural or liturgical themes. For example, the Episcopal Diocese of West Texas has an online planning resource that develops a monthly stewardship theme linked to the liturgical season. It suggests ways to connect each month's theme with spiritual growth, ministry activities, missional priorities, personal and congregational finances, and creation care.[3]

Preaching

Because of our cultural aversion to talking about money, many pastors avoid preaching on the subject except on that *one* Sunday when they hold their noses and steel themselves to deliver *the* dreaded stewardship sermon. Or they foist the job off on a guest preacher to avoid putting themselves on the hot seat. The problem with this approach is that congregants tune out the message because it is perceived as a fund-raising pitch, or they know to stay home that day.

Nurturing a culture of generosity and a sound understanding of biblical stewardship requires ongoing, persistent effort. The Christian message regarding how we should live in relation to our money and possessions is liberating and transformative. But it is also profoundly countercultural. Inviting people to step away from their cultural beliefs about money and giving requires ongoing spiritual formation. In our culture of affluence and overconsumption, this is arguably the greatest spiritual challenge facing the church in North America and other developed nations.

Preachers should strive to integrate stewardship themes into their preaching throughout the year when the subjects of generosity and living in right relationship to our things arise in relation to other spiritual messages, not just when their stated topic is money or giving. Fortunately, there are many fine books and resources to assist preachers in connecting stewardship themes with different biblical texts, the lectionary cycle, and the liturgical calendar. In *Preaching and Stewardship*, Craig Satterlee gives three invaluable tips: (1) let Jesus do the talking; (2) appeal to people's better selves; and (3) don't coerce or command.[4]

GETTING STARTED

The goal of establishing a year-round stewardship ministry may seem daunting. But the wonderful thing is that you can start small. Remember that not every aspect of a well-rounded stewardship program needs to happen on an annual basis, especially in a smaller church. Any church can take a step forward by simply adding something new. Preach a sermon series on a stewardship-related theme at a time of year totally apart from when you're asking people to make pledges or conduct a thank-a-thon to acknowledge the importance of supporting the church's mission. But without taking the time to consider your options and plan, such opportunities will pass you by.

Chapter 20

Leadership for Stewardship

Given financial pressures on churches, pastors and lay leadership can easily get anxious and look for quick and easy solutions. Even though it is hard to accept, times of challenge require going back to the basics of leadership regarding stewardship and church finances. Strong youth programs do not happen quickly nor do splendid music programs, prayer ministries, or community service. All require the use of tested leadership methods that take focus and time. Matters of financial generosity and stability are no exceptions. Such leadership requires going back to the basics of what we know about all effective leadership. Leading a church to a strong stewardship ethic and solid church finances require four elements of all fruitful leadership—vision, team, culture, and integrity.[1]

VISION

The single most common theme in all studies of leadership is the presence of a powerful shared vision. A vision is a picture of a preferred future to which we believe God is calling us. Churches are strong when they lead with vision—when people are asked to link their personal vision of discipleship with the vision God has given the congregation to fulfill.

How does vision relate to giving? Put simply it is everything. A vision is all we ever have to offer people when we seek giving in the church. You want to say that as a community of faith we believe that God has called us to be the presence of Christ at the moment and in this place in this way. You are inviting people to join a dream of God's preferred future for themselves, their congregation, and others. In essence, as a community of believers, you

155

are saying that "we have a dream" of a world far closer to God's will than the current state of things.

We are not asking people to help an institution survive, or even become stronger, but to give that, through a human institution, all humanity may come to know the abundant life God wishes for all through Jesus Christ. And so it is that we are inviting people to give to bring about a future that is better than today. We are inviting people to give to a dream that, as Langston Hughes put it, "never has been yet—And yet must be." We are not asking people to give to pay utility bills or fix leaking roofs. We are asking people to give to a dream—that the hungry are fed, that the sick healed, that the imprisoned are visited, and that the naked clothed. That is why we ask. That is why we seek money.

In the early days of a new church-related school, the president went to a local bank for a $50,000 loan. The banker asked about collateral. The president, expecting the question, promptly gathered from his pocket a handful of pledge cards representing gift commitments from church members interested in the new school. The banker, after a moment, responded, "Let's be honest. With all due respect, all you have is a dream." So it is with all faith leaders.

Mary McLeod Bethune, the daughter of former slaves, achieved much in education and civil rights. In 1904 she began a boarding school for African American girls with reportedly only $1.50 and faith in God. Her school later became a college and now continues as the co-educational Bethune-Cookman University in Daytona Beach, Florida. One way she financed her school was through baking pies and selling them. It was through this activity that she met several influential businessmen, including James Gamble of Proctor & Gamble. She told Gamble about her new school and the first building named Faith Hall. She asked him to become a trustee. He agreed to visit. When Gamble arrived one morning in his limousine, he looked around a desolate area that had once been a garbage dump. He saw one dilapidated shed, some girls working and some other girls reading, and Bethune coming to greet him. "Where is this school you want me to be a trustee of," he asked. Bethune replied, "I'm asking you to be a trustee of a school that exists only in my mind." Gamble responded, "This is the first time I've been asked to be the trustee of a dream. I hope I am worthy."[2]

We are not asking for money. We are asking people to become trustees, stewards, sponsors of a dream for the world that exists only in the mind and heart and soul of God. Church leaders can boldly say that our church exists for you but also to give you a chance to join in God's dream of a new heaven and a new earth.

TEAM

A second element of effective leadership is team. The question here is, "Given the church's vision, who are the people without whom this vision cannot become a reality?" Certainly leaders must relate to everyone. For the sake of the mission, however, leaders must give a particular kind of attention to the people required to make the vision a reality.

Nowhere is this truer than in financial giving. When we have a vision with a major financial goal, we simply have to say, "Given this challenge, who are those without whom it cannot become a reality?" We need to plan to involve everyone, but we need to find a special way to involve early and often those people of whom much is being asked and without whom the challenge will not be met. This is not to exclude anyone from any vision. Rather, as those in the initial core group become closer to the vision themselves, they can help to find ways to involve everyone else.

Such teams are democratic in that they are shaped by the vision. The team for the church's financial goals when the vision to start a neighborhood drama group to serve the community will be different than when the vision is to begin a congregational prayer ministry. Those "without whom the vision cannot become a reality" will depend on the church's vision. But everyone in your church can be part of the vision and will probably be needed for your church to reach its full potential.

This "team" is not necessarily a formal committee. It may have its start in the mind of the leader giving oversight. It will include many of the key people from existing committees as well as those who are not on such committees but whose support is essential to the goal. It may also involve someone from another congregation whose volunteer consulting is needed for a new way of doing things.

You begin not with everyone but with a subset of the congregation and go out from there. Some visualize this as widening the group through concentric circles or layered concentric circles. You begin with the small circle—the most committed and the most essential. Then this team is able to move out to all stakeholders. Each year the team must achieve two financial goals—meeting the near-term financial needs and building for the future. Sometimes we make the mistake of attending to one and ignoring the other. If reaching the year's financial goal is the only focus, you run the risk of not extending the circle of generosity to include new people. On the other hand, if all the focus is on new commitments, then that goal may be reached but not the financial needs because of inadequate attention being paid to securing larger gifts, which may be the financial foundation of your church.

It is important to pay proper attention both to people with a demonstrated history of giving and to people who have yet to take the first step in stewardship. Doing so will serve your congregation well and help all members grow in discipleship. There is a place for everyone in the church but that does not mean everyone is spiritually qualified for leadership. A history of exemplary stewardship should be a requirement for top leadership positions. If your financial leadership do not lead in stewardship, the message to the congregation is that giving is not so important. Choose spiritually mature leaders and others will follow them and aspire to be like them.

CULTURE

Another element of effective leadership is culture. The question here is, "How do we communicate the vision throughout the organization's culture?" Culture is simply "who we are and how we do things around here." It is the ethos, language, stories, space, symbols, heroes, recognitions, and daily routines. Culture is important because it is here that the vision becomes a reality—if it does at all. It is in the culture that the vision jumps off the page and comes alive, in the same way a movie makes a script come alive. You may have read the script, but it is a very different experience to see the movie.

Why is this important for giving? Because people rarely make their decisions based on an objective assessment of facts. Their decisions are shaped by all the images, stories, and feelings they associate with your church. Remember people "hear" what they "see." What do people see at your church during the year? We must regularly ask, "How do we communicate the church's vision and the vision of joyful generosity throughout the congregation's culture?"

We must find ways to help that script come alive through symbols and celebrations that people will remember. Our neglect of culture is often the reason we find ourselves saying, "Why don't people give more? We are doing such good work." Could it be that despite having the clear mission, careful documentation for our programs and budget, and pertinent statistics to demonstrate our needs, we have not found ways to move these realities off the page of the script and onto the movie of the culture?

Here are some examples:

- People may not remember the figures on the financial update, but they remember that "my church shares information."
- They may not remember what country is featured this month on the Missions bulletin board, but they remember that "we are a church in mission."
- They may not know the name of the child that talks about what Vacation Bible School meant to her, but they will remember the child.

- They may read in the bulletin that the annual audit is complete and available in the church office and never pick up a copy, but they will remember that someone's "minding the store."

Rather than putting all your focus on literature to distribute during a stewardship campaign, think about opportunities throughout the year for people to experience the vision so that it becomes more a part of their understanding of the church. Often because of our reluctance to think about giving except when necessity requires it, we miss so many opportunities for people to experience the movie scripted in the pages we hand out that are easily ignored or forgotten. The realization of a vision does not come from any one effort but the accumulated cultural expressions of that vision throughout the year.

INTEGRITY

Leadership for giving must be characterized by integrity. Such integrity not only includes the personal integrity of its pastoral, stewardship, and finance leaders but also includes the organizational integrity of the congregation.

More is expected of leaders not because we are talking about the church but because we are talking about leadership. All leaders draw strength from personal integrity. We are not speaking of perfection but of consistency and coherence. The personal integrity question for all leaders is, "Are you willing to wear the vision you represent the way people wear clothes?" To the extent this is the case, there is strength. When such behavior is not the case, there is weakness. So in generous congregations the church leaders wear the vision of joyful generosity in proportion to their ability and resources.

John Wesley is known for things he said about giving. In his time, he was equally known for his example of giving. He once told his sister, "Money never stays with me. It would burn me if it did. I throw it out of my hands as soon as possible, lest it should find its way into my heart."[3] Earlier he had said that "if I leave behind me ten pounds (above my debts, and the little arrears of my fellowship), you and all mankind bear witness against me 'that I lived and died a thief and a robber.'"[4]

In addition to the essential personal integrity of all leaders, integrity also includes the institutional integrity of the church. Organizational integrity includes the fundamental integrity built into systems of receiving, handling, distributing, and accounting for funds covered elsewhere. But there is much more. Again, the integrity issue for the churches is the same as for its leaders—consistency and coherence. Is there consistency between what we say we are, what people perceive us to be, and what an objective assessment of reality would say we are? Is there harmony? Do people experience us as being what we say we are?

The credibility of the church and its leaders will influence giving far more than a brochure about the church's budget. Such credibility cannot be separated from the quality of relationships among leaders and members. Indeed, a secular term for fund-raising is "development." The word "development" is not just a euphemism for fund-raising. Development is an accurate description of leadership for giving; we are about developing relationships—out of which comes trust—out of which comes giving.

Not only must the church show systemic integrity in how funds are handled and used, it must also show integrity in living the vision it proclaims. We are not talking about a church being good or bad so much as living what you say you are. For example, you do not have to put on your bulletin the mantra, "In the heart of the city with the city on our heart." But, if you do, then integrity requires that you live out these words, not perfectly but so much so that both members and visitors quickly discover your commitment to the city.

The credibility essential for fruitful leadership at the personal and organizational levels is earned slowly. It grows day by day. It can be lost quickly. Churches and their leaders need to understand the power of their integrity and how shattering its compromise can be.

CONCLUSION

Over 200 years ago, the French educator Alexis de Tocqueville came to study America. In *Democracy in America*, he wrote about seeing the best educated, freest, and happiest people he had encountered anywhere in the world. But he also noted a cloud hanging over them. They "never stop thinking of the good things they have not got." He then commented, "They clutch everything and hold nothing fast."[5]

When we ask people to give, we are inviting people who may be desperately clutching at many things to hold fast to something important. The Bible does not say accumulate all the things you can and then receive the kingdom of God but rather seek the kingdom of God and all these other things begin to fall in place. Remember the story of James Gamble and Mary McLeod Bethune. Here was one of the wealthiest men in the United States who could have clutched anything, and yet it was Mary McLeod Bethune who gave him something he could hold fast.

Appendix A

The Three Funds

Three types of budgets represent categories of income and expenditures that are normally needed to carry out a congregation's mission—the operating fund, the capital renewal and replacement fund, and the endowment fund. While the operating fund is essential, the capital renewal and replacement fund is equally essential if a congregation owns any facilities; however, it is not always present. The endowment fund is the least present in congregations and regarded as a luxury (or even a detriment) by some congregations, although when well planned and managed such a fund can enhance a church's ministry.

Operating Fund

Purpose	Annual operating financial needs.
Defining characteristic	Covers ministry expenses incurred and used within the year.
Sources of income	The primary source is ongoing giving of tithes and offerings (pledged or unpledged) by members.
	Other sources of income include fund raisers, special offerings, rental income, fee income, gifts in kind, and memorial gifts, among others. Churches are increasingly viewing the funding of their operating budgets coming from multiple streams of income and not just the offering plate.

(Continued)

Operating Fund Continued

Cautions	When budgeting for income, keep in mind that the operating budget should be funded by recurring and relatively predictable income. Therefore, you want to avoid using bequests or other large onetime gifts for operating expenses. If such funds are required for operations, then you are just putting off the day when you must address the gap between recurring income and recurring expenses. In the case of bequests, it is wise to resist the use of such a "lifetime" gift for purposes that have such a short life span, whereas such gifts going to either capital purposes or endowment will assure that the gift makes possible something with a life longer than one year.
	Set budgets that are both realistic and visionary. Congregations need to be stretched, but it is discouraging and ultimately self-defeating continually to adopt budgets for which even if members give much more than the year before, there is no chance of reaching the budget goal.

Capital Fund (or Building Fund)

Purpose	New building, renovation, and major repairs or replacements.
Defining characteristic	Covers capital projects with a life longer than one year.
Sources of income (stable environment)	If a church does not have to take on a major building project, this church should develop several sources of income to provide a financial foundation for the inevitable capital expenses that come with existing facilities (replacing roofs, computers, and equipment; painting; and renovation) as well as any new facilities that may be needed.
	Some sources for funding this fund include special gifts, memorials, bequest income, fund raisers, designating a percentage of the operating budget to be transferred to this fund each year, and sale of property.
Sources of income (growing environment)	A church facing an immediate need to build will need to do what churches have typically done to meet such major capital needs: have a capital campaign and borrow funds.
	The source of funding in this case becomes the cash raised or pledged from the capital campaign and a debt line in the operating budget.

Key plans required	To make the Capital Fund work, the trustees or comparable officers in consultation with a broad network of church leaders need to prepare and revise annually a five-year capital projected budget. They begin by listing the categories of capital expenditures that are recurring, even if not every year. Such things include painting, roof replacement, technology replacements, and basic equipment replacement. There may be other projects that need to be on the list such as upgrades to some facilities or renovations. There may be some onetime projects on the list. Then, they make their best estimates of what expenditures will be needed and in what years over the next five years (perhaps ten years). This permits the congregation to see what the capital priorities are. It also gives an idea of how much capital funding will be needed each year. These projections will change. For example, if a roof replacement is scheduled for a particular year and when that year arrives the roof is still in good shape, then that expense is moved ahead a year or so and other projects can be done that year. Keep in mind that any capital needs that deal with health and safety issues must always be moved to the top of the list and have immediate priority.
Cautions	Because of constant pressure to meet operating budgets, churches often act as if they will have no capital expenses. Then, when such expenses come along in the form of a leaking roof or a furnace that must be replaced, there has to be a special appeal or funds have to be drawn from the operating budget, normally meaning that the operating budget is thrown in the red for the year.

Permanent Fund or Endowment

Purpose	Invested permanent funds providing continuing support for purposes designated by the donor or by congregation policy
Defining characteristic	Principal is invested and earnings (interest, dividends, and appreciation) spent based on an approved spending policy for approved purposes. An endowment is made up of funds designated for endowment by the donor and other funds placed there by the governing body (technically "quasi-endowment"). The governing body can choose later to use these funds differently.

(Continued)

Permanent Fund or Endowment Continued

Sources of income	The primary source of endowment income for many churches is from bequests of members. Other sources of income include special designated gifts, memorials, sale of property, larger onetime gifts, and reinvested funds for the purpose of maintaining the purchasing power of the endowment in the face of inflation.
Key decisions to be made	**Bequests policy.** All churches need a bequest policy. The policy acknowledges that designated bequests, if accepted, will be used for the intended purpose and then explain what happens with undesignated bequest income. For example, the policy may specify that half goes to the capital fund and half to endowment. Of course, the percentages could be different, or all could go to one or the other fund.
	Investment policy. Most churches have access to denominational foundations that invest funds for churches. These foundations offer a variety of investment portfolios with reasonable fees. Growing the fund requires a strong position in equities.
	Spending policy. Your goal is to have a steady and predictable flow of income for ministries without eroding the value of the initial gifts. To accomplish these purposes, you will need a conservative spending rate. You want your total return (interest, dividends, and appreciation) over a typical multiyear period to cover inflation plus your spending rate to preserve the buying power of the endowment and also fund ministry. So, if you assume a total return on average of 7 percent and an inflation rate of 3 percent, then a spending rate of 4 percent will work. You need to monitor all these rates and adjust as needed.
	Approved purposes for endowment expenditures. Determine where endowment can do the most good to strengthen the church to serve in the future. Of course, funds given for specified purposes (e.g., youth) are used for that purpose. One can always justify endowment funds going to the Capital Fund because this fund invests in enhancements to facilities that will serve the congregation for years into the future. The same is true if funds are used to pay debt from prior enhancements. Children's ministry and youth ministry build for the future. Mission ministries that engage the congregation with its community strengthen the church's future.
Cautions	• Many are reluctant to establish endowment funds for fear that it will decrease giving by members. If handled properly, this does not have to happen. Be transparent in all matters related to the endowment. Be forthright about what it funds and what it does not fund. Issue reports.
	• Do not see the endowment as a subsidy to cover operating fund deficits. If that is how your endowment is currently being used, see if you can begin withdrawing from this use of the endowment.
	• Resist a high spending rate. A lower spending rate means that there will almost always be some increase in funds available from year to year, and the endowment will continue to grow.

Appendix B

Sample Capital Budget Worksheet

Before beginning: Study your capital renewal and replacement needs through extensive conversations and inspections.

Step 1: From all the work you have done thus far, you are now ready to make a list of current and future needs. It will be a long list but, at this point, do not worry about the length. You are trying to capture a comprehensive picture of your needs.

Step 2: Once you have your full list of needs, you need to organize them into subject categories.

Template List and Categories	
Step 1—Identify Capital Needs	*Step 2—Categorize*
Health, safety, code compliance	**Roofs**
Accessibility	**Painting**

(Continued)

Template List and Categories		

Step 1—Identify Capital Needs	*Step 2—Categorize*	
	Major systems (heating/cooling)	**Renovation**
	Technology/sound systems	**New construction**
	Equipment and furnishings	

Step 3: Next, think about project sequencing.

First, place the highest priority projects in year one. Health, safety, and code compliance come first.

Second, divide large projects into units so that they can be spread across multiple years.

Third, add cost estimates to each project.

Please note that, if a church is doing full generally accepted accounting standards (GAAP) accounting, you will need additional information such as the date purchased, useful life, salvage value, and vendor. This information will be needed to calculate depreciation amounts.

Template Price and Schedule									
Step 3—Prioritize, Schedule with Costs									
Year 1	*Cost*	*Year 2*	*Cost*	*Year 3*	*Cost*	*Year 4*	*Cost*	*Year 5*	*Cost*

Template Price and Schedule									
Step 3—Prioritize, Schedule with Costs									
Year 1	Cost	Year 2	Cost	Year 3	Cost	Year 4	Cost	Year 5	Cost
Total	$		$		$		$		$

Bibliography

Allison, Chelsea. "Checking Out: A Brief History of Checks." *Fin*, March 1, 2019. https://fin.plaid.com/articles/checking-out-a-brief-history-of-checks.

Amerson, Melvin. *Stewardship in African-American Churches: A New Paradigm*. Nashville, TN: Upper Room, 2015.

Amerson, Melvin, and James Amerson. *Celebrate the Offering*. Nashville, TN: Discipleship Resources, 2007.

Arrillaga-Andreessen, Laura. *Giving 2.0: Transform Your Giving and Our World*. San Francisco, CA: Jossey-Bass, 2012.

Berlin, Tom. *The Generous Church: A Guide for Pastors*. Nashville, TN: Abingdon Press, 2016.

Berneking, Nate. *The Vile Practices of Church Leadership: Finance and Administration*. Nashville, TN: Abingdon Press, 2017.

Brueggemann, Walter. *Money and Possessions*. Louisville, KY: Westminster John Knox Press, 2016.

Carter, Kenneth H., and Audrey Warren. *Fresh Expressions: A New Kind of Methodist Church for People Not in Church*. Nashville, TN: Abingdon Press, 2017.

"Charitable Giving Statistics." *Nonprofits Source*. https://nonprofitssource.com/online-giving-statistics.

Chaves, Mark, and Sharon L. Miller, eds. *Financing American Religion*. Walnut Creek, CA: AltaMira Press, 1999.

Christopher, J. Clif. *Not Your Parents' Offering Plate: A New Vision for Financial Stewardship*. Nashville, TN: Abingdon Press, 2008.

Christopher, J. Clif. *Rich Church, Poor Church: Keys to Effective Financial Ministry*. Nashville, TN: Abingdon Press, 2012.

Cloughen, Charles, Jr. *One-Minute Stewardship: Creative Ways to Talk about Money in Church*. New York: Church Publishing, 2018.

Cormode, D. Scott. *Making Spiritual Sense: Christian Leaders as Spiritual Interpreters*. Eugene, OR: Wipf and Stock, 2013.

Daniels, Joe, and Christie Latona. *Connecting for a Change: How to Engage People, Churches, and Partners to Inspire Hope in Your Community.* Nashville, TN: Abingdon Press, 2019.

De Lea, Brittany. "Get Ready for One of the Greatest Wealth Transfers in History." *New York Post*, March 13, 2018. https://nypost.com/2018/03/13/get-ready-for-one-of-the-greatest-wealth-transfers-in-history.

DeYmaz, Mark. *The Coming Revolution in Church Economics.* Grand Rapids, MI: Baker Books, 2019.

DeYmaz, Mark. (*The Coming Revolution in Church Economics*) Interview by Ann Michel. *Leading Ideas Talks*, Podcast audio, episode 55, May 13, 2020. https://www.churchleadership.com/podcast/episode-55-the-coming-revolution-in-church-economics-featuring-mark-deymaz.

DeYmaz, Mark. *Disruption: Repurposing the Church to Redeem the Community.* New York: Harper Collins, 2017.

Dropkin, Murray, Jim Halpin, and Bill La Touche. *The Budget-Building Book for Nonprofits: A Step-by-Step Guide for Managers and Boards.* 2nd ed. San Francisco, CA: Jossey-Bass, 2008.

Durall, Michael. *Beyond the Offering Plate.* Nashville, TN: Abingdon Press, 2003.

Follett, Mary Parker. *Freedom and Co-Ordination: Lectures in Business Organization.* London: Management Publication Trust, 1949.

Fullerton, Barbara. "Growing Generosity: Identity as Stewards in the United Church of Canada." Doctoral thesis, Wesley Theological Seminary, Washington, DC, 2009.

Golv, John L. *Our Stewardship: Managing Our Assets.* Minneapolis, MN: Augsburg Fortress, 2002.

Hall, Eddy, Ray Bowman, and J. Skipp Machmer. *The More-with-Less Church: Maximize Your Money, Space, Time, and People to Multiply Ministry Impact.* Grand Rapids, MI: Baker Books, 2014.

Hamilton, Adam. *Enough: Discovering Joy through Simplicity and Generosity*, revised and updated. Nashville, TN: Abingdon Press, 2012.

Harnish, James A. *Earn. Save. Give. Wesley's Simple Rules on Money.* Nashville, TN: Abingdon Press, 2015.

Heikes, Laura. "Mature Disciples Supporting New Givers." *Leading Ideas*, August 31, 2011. https://www.churchleadership.com/leading-ideas/mature-disciples-supporting-new-givers

Heikes, Laura. "Spending More on Others Fosters Increased Generosity." *Leading Ideas*, March 26, 2014. https://www.churchleadership.com/leading-ideas/spending-more-on-others-fosters-increased-generosity.

Hoge, Dean R., Patrick McNamara, and Charles Zech. *Plain Talk about Churches and Money.* Lanham, MD: Rowman & Littlefield, 1997.

Hoge, Dean R., Charles E. Zech, Patrick H. McNamara, and Michael J. Donahue. *Money Matters: Personal Giving in American Churches.* Louisville, KY: Westminster John Knox Press, 1996.

Hotchkiss, Dan. *Ministry and Money: A Guide for Clergy and Their Friends.* Lanham, MD: Rowman & Littlefield, 2002.

Hudnut-Beumler, James. *Generous Saints: Congregations Rethinking Ethics and Money.* Lanham, MD: Rowman & Littlefield, 1999.

Hudnut-Beumler, James. *In Pursuit of the Almighty's Dollar*. Chapel Hill, NC: University of North Carolina Press, 2007.

Jamieson, Janet T., and Philip D. Jamieson. *Ministry and Money: A Practical Guide for Pastors*. Louisville, KY: John Knox Press, 2009.

Jeavons, Thomas H., and Rebekah Burch Basinger. *Growing Giver's Hearts*. San Francisco, CA: Jossey-Bass, 2000.

Jones, Jeffrey M. "Majority in U.S. Do Not Have a Will." *Gallup*, May 18, 2016. https://news.gallup.com/poll/191651/majority-not.aspx.

Jones-Smith, Jacqueline. "Thinking Outside the Box: Finances for African American Churches Conference." Presentation at Wesley Theological Seminary, Washington, DC, November 2, 2019.

Keucher, Gerald W. *Remember the Future: Financial Leadership and Asset Management for Congregations*. New York: Church Publishing, 2006.

King, David P., Brad R. Fulton, Christopher W. Munn, and Jamie L. Goodwin. *National Study of Congregations' Economic Practices*. Indiana: Lake Institute on Faith & Giving, Indiana University Lilly Family School of Philanthropy, 2019.

Lane, Charles R. *Ask, Thank, Tell: Improving Stewardship Ministry in Your Congregation*. Minneapolis, MN: Augsburg Fortress, 2006.

MacDonald, G. Jeffrey. *Part-Time Is Plenty: Thriving without Full-Time Clergy*. Louisville, KY: Westminster John Knox Press, 2020.

Malotky, Catherine. "How a Strategically Planned Stewardship Campaign Increased Giving." *Leading Ideas*, August 7, 2019. https://www.churchleadership.com/leading-ideas/how-a-strategically-planned-stewardship-campaign-increased-giving.

Marcuson, Margaret. *Money and Your Ministry*. Portland, OR: Marcuson Leadership Circle, 2014.

McAllister Wilson, David. "Why Clergy Personal Finances Matter." *Leading Ideas*, October 21, 2015. https://www.churchleadership.com/leading-ideas/why-clergy-personal-finances-matter.

McNamara, Patrick H. *More than Money: Portraits of Transformative Stewardship*. Lanham, MD: Rowman & Littlefield, 1999.

Meeks, M. Douglas. *God the Economist: The Doctrine of God and Political Economy*. Minneapolis, MN: Fortress Press, 1989.

Miller, Herb. *New Consecration Sunday Stewardship Program*, revised edition. Nashville, TN: Abingdon Press, 2007.

Moore, Waveney Ann. "Christ United Methodist Selling Its Parking Lot in Hot Downtown St. Petersburg Market." *Tampa Bay Times*, December 20, 2017. https://www.tampabay.com/news/business/economicdevelopment/Christ-United-Methodist-selling-its-parking-lot-in-hot-downtown-St-Petersburg-market_163504218.

Moore, Waveney Ann. "From Tiny Downtown Parking Lot, St. Pete Church Blessed with Millions." *Tampa Bay Times*, March 4, 2020. https://www.tampabay.com/news/st-petersburg/2020/03/04/from-tiny-downtown-parking-lot-st-pete-church-blessed-with-millions.

Mosser, David N. *Stewardship Services*. Nashville, TN: Abingdon Press, 2007.

National Congregations Study, Cumulative Dataset, 2012. http://www.thearda.com/ConQS/qs_295.asp.

Nouwen, Henri J. M. *A Spirituality of Fundraising*. Nashville, TN: Upper Room Books, 2010.

Orr, C. J., and Devon McCann. "The $30 Trillion 'Great Wealth Transfer'—Some Planned Giving Tools to Help Nonprofits Benefit." *NonProfit Pro*, October 16, 2018. https://www.nonprofitpro.com/post/the-30-trillion-great-wealth-transfer-some-planned-giving-tools-to-help-nonprofits-benefit.

"Our Story." Shawnee Community Christian Church. Accessed date June 7, 2020. https://shawneecommunity.org/our-story/.

Perry, Sarah. "Morganton: Open Hearts Bakery." *Our State*, March 28, 2013. https://www.ourstate.com/open-hearts-bakery-morganton.

Phillips, Matt. "The Spectacular Decline of Checks." *The Atlantic*, June 5, 2014. https://www.theatlantic.com/business/archive/2014/06/the-rise-and-fall-of-checks/372217.

Picardo, Rosario. *Funding Ministry with Five Loaves and Two Fishes*. Nashville, TN: Abingdon Press, 2016.

Pomrenke, Lee Ann M. "Closing a Congregation as an Act of Faithfulness." *Leading Ideas*, February 7, 2018. https://www.churchleadership.com/leading-ideas/closing-a-congregation-as-an-act-of-faithfulness.

Ponting, David M. *From Scarcity to Abundance*. Harrisburg, PA: Morehouse Publishing, 2005.

Powell, Mark Allan. *Giving to God: The Bible's Good News about Living a Generous Life*. Grand Rapids, MI: Eerdmans Publishing, 2006.

Robinson, Anthony B. *Stewardship for Vital Congregations*. Cleveland, OH: Pilgrim Press, 2011.

Rogers, Richard. *The E-Giving Guide for Every Church: Using Digital Tools to Grow Ministry*. Nashville, TN: Abingdon Press, 2016.

Satterlee, Craig A. *Preaching and Stewardship*. Lanham, MD: Rowman & Littlefield, 2011.

Schaff, Terry, and Doug Schaff. *The Fundraising Planner: A Working Model for Raising the Dollars You Need*. San Francisco, CA: Jossey-Bass, 1999.

Searcy, Nelson. *Maximize: How to Develop Extravagant Givers in Your Church*. Grand Rapids, MI: Baker Books, 2010.

Skjegstad, Joy. "Are Grants the Answer?" *Faith and Leadership*, July 6, 2009. https://faithandleadership.com/are-grants-answer.

Skjegstad, Joy. *Starting a Nonprofit at Your Church*. Lanham, MD: Rowman & Littlefield, 2002.

Skjegstad, Joy. *Winning Grants to Strengthen Your Ministry*. Lanham, MD: Rowman & Littlefield, 2007.

Slaughter, Mike. *The Christian Wallet: Spending, Giving, and Living with a Conscience*. Louisville, KY: Westminster John Knox Press, 2016.

Slaughter, Mike. *Christmas Is Not Your Birthday: Experience the Joy of Living and Giving Like Jesus*. Nashville, TN: Abingdon Press, 2011.

Slaughter, Michael. *Money Matters: Financial Freedom for all God's Churches*. Nashville, TN: Abingdon Press, 2006.

Smith, Amy Symens, and Edward Trevelyan. "In Some States, More than Half of Older Residents Live in Rural Areas." U.S. Census Bureau, October 22, 2019.

https://www.census.gov/library/stories/2019/10/older-population-in-rural-america.html.

Smith, Christian, and Hillary Davidson. *The Paradox of Generosity*. New York: Oxford University Press, 2014.

Smith, Christian, Michael O. Emerson, and Patricia Snell. *Passing the Plate: Why American Christians Don't Give Away More Money*. New York: Oxford University Press, 2008.

Tatenhove, Krin Van, and Rob Mueller. *Neighborhood Church: Transforming Your Congregation into a Powerhouse for Mission*. Louisville, KY: Westminster John Knox Press, 2019.

Teasdale, Mark. *Go! How to Become a Great Commission Church*. Nashville, TN: General Board of Higher Education and Ministry, 2017.

Tennant, Matthew. *Preaching in Plenty and in Want*. Valley Forge, PA: Judson Press, 2011.

Thumma, Scott. "Becoming a Virtual Faith Community: Applying Past Data to New Ideas." *Faith Communities Today*, March 30, 2020. https://faithcommunitiestoday.org/becoming-a-virtual-faith-community-applying-past-data-to-new-ideas.

Towner, Dick, and John Tofilon. *Good Sense Budget Course*. Grand Rapids, MI: Zondervan, 2002.

U.S. Census Bureau. "New Census Data Show Differences between Urban and Rural Populations." December 8, 2016. Release number CB16–210. https://www.census.gov/newsroom/press-releases/2016/cb16-210.html.

Vargo, Richard J., and Vonna Laue. *Essential Guide to Church Finances*. Carol Stream, IL: Your Church Resources, 2009.

Weems, Cynthia D. "Online Giving Connects Ministry and Mission." *Leading Ideas*, March 27, 2013. https://www.churchleadership.com/leading-ideas/online-giving-connects-ministry-and-mission.

Weems, Lovett H., Jr. *Church Leadership: Vision, Team, Culture, and Integrity*, revised edition. Nashville, TN: Abingdon Press, 2010.

Wheeler, Sondra Ely. *Wealth as Peril and Obligation: The New Testament on Possessions*. Grand Rapids, MI: Eerdmans Publishing, 1995.

Willard, Chris, and Jim Sheppard. *Contagious Generosity: Creating a Culture of Giving in Your Church*. Grand Rapids, MI: Zondervan, 2012.

Williams, Sidney S. Jr. *Fishing Differently: Ministry Formation in the Marketplace*. Apopka, FL: Certa Publishing, 2018.

Wimberly, John W., Jr. *The Business of the Church*. Lanham, MD: Rowman & Littlefield, 2010.

Witherington, Ben III. *Jesus and Money: A Guide for Times of Financial Crisis*. Grand Rapids, MI: Brazos Press, 2010.

Wright, Lauren Tyler. *Giving the Sacred Art: Creating a Lifestyle of Generosity*. Woodstock, VT: SkyLight Paths Publishing, 2008.

Wuthnow, Robert. *The Crisis in the Churches: Spiritual Malaise, Fiscal Woe*. New York: Oxford University Press, 1997.

Zehring, John and Kate Jagger. *Beyond Stewardship: A Church Guide to Generous Giving Campaigns*. Valley Forge, PA: Judson Press, 2016.

Zinsmeister, Karl. "Less God, Less Giving?" *Philanthropy Magazine*, Winter 2019.

Notes

CHAPTER 1

1. Ben Witherington III, *Jesus and Money: A Guide for Times of Financial Crisis* (Grand Rapids, MI: Brazos Press, 2010), 46.
2. David King et al., *National Study of Congregations' Economic Practices* (Indiana: Lake Institute on Faith and Giving, 2019), 25.
3. Molly Phinney Baskette, *Real Good Church* (Cleveland, OH: Pilgrim Press, 2014), 100.

CHAPTER 2

1. All scriptural citations are from the New Revised Standard Version of the Bible unless otherwise noted.
2. Mark Allan Powell, *Giving to God: The Bible's Good News about Living a Generous Life* (Grand Rapids, MI: Eerdmans Publishing, 2006), 41.
3. Christian Smith and Hillary Davidson, *The Paradox of Generosity* (New York: Oxford University Press, 2014), 12.
4. Christian Smith, Michael O. Emerson, and Patricia Snell, *Passing the Plate: Why American Christians Don't Give Away More Money* (New York: Oxford University Press, 2008), 27.
5. Ibid., 11.
6. Ibid., 52–53.
7. Laura Heikes, "Spending More on Others Fosters Increased Generosity," *Leading Ideas E-Newsletter*, March 26, 2014, https://www.churchleadership.com/leading-ideas/spending-more-on-others-fosters-increased-generosity/.
8. Karl Zinsmeister, "Less God, Less Giving?" *Philanthropy Magazine* (Winter 2019).
9. Mike Slaughter, *Christmas Is Not Your Birthday: Experience the Joy of Living and Giving Like Jesus* (Nashville, TN: Abingdon Press, 2011), xi.

CHAPTER 3

1. Craig A. Satterlee, *Preaching and Stewardship* (Lanham, MD: Rowman & Littlefield, 2011), xii–iii.
2. Powell, *Giving to God*, 10–11.
3. Gerald W. Keucher, *Remember the Future: Financial Leadership and Asset Management for Congregations* (New York: Church Publishing, 2006), 142.
4. Smith, Emerson, and Snell, *Passing the Plate*, 63.
5. Ibid., 66–67.
6. Ibid., 11.
7. Satterlee, *Preaching and Stewardship*, 59–60.
8. Smith, Emerson, and Snell, *Passing the Plate*, 183.
9. Satterlee, *Preaching and Stewardship*, 96.
10. Smith, Emerson, and Snell, *Passing the Plate*, 43–44.
11. Witherington, *Jesus and Money*, 21.
12. Ibid.
13. James Hudnut-Beumler, *In Pursuit of the Almighty's Dollar* (Chapel Hill, NC: University of North Carolina Press, 2007), 50–55.

CHAPTER 4

1. Smith, Emerson, and Snell, *Passing the Plate*, 95.
2. Ibid.
3. Ibid.
4. Ibid., 94.
5. King et al., *National Study of Congregations' Economic Practices*, 21.
6. Ibid.
7. Ibid.
8. Smith, Emerson, and Snell, *Passing the Plate*, 105.

CHAPTER 5

1. Smith, Emerson, and Snell, *Passing the Plate*, 29.
2. Laura Heikes, "Mature Disciples Supporting New Givers," *Leading Ideas E-Newsletter*, August 31, 2011, https://www.churchleadership.com/leading-ideas/mature-disciples-supporting-new-givers/.
3. Catherine Malotky, "How a Strategically Planned Stewardship Campaign Increased Giving," *Leading Ideas E-Newsletter*, August 7, 2019, https://www.churchleadership.com/leading-ideas/how-a-strategically-planned-stewardship-campaign-increased-giving/.

CHAPTER 6

1. Claire Greene, Marcin Hitczenko, Brian Prescott, and Oz Shy, "U.S. Consumers' Use of Personal Checks," Federal Reserve Bank of Atlanta, February 10, 2020, 2, https://www.frbatlanta.org/-/media/documents/banking/consumer-payments/research-data-reports/2020/02/13/us-consumers-use-of-personal-checks-evidence-from-a-diary-survey/rdr2001.pdf.
2. Matt Phillips, "The Spectacular Decline of Checks," *The Atlantic* (Atlantic Media Company), June 5, 2014, https://www.theatlantic.com/business/archive/2014/06/the-rise-and-fall-of-checks/372217/). Chelsea Allison, "Checking Out: A Brief History of Checks," *Fin* (Fin | Insights on the Future of Finance from Plaid), March 13, 2019, https://fin.plaid.com/articles/checking-out-a-brief-history-of-checks/.
3. King et al., *National Study of Congregations' Economic Practices*, 18–19.
4. Ibid., 19.
5. Scott Thumma, "Becoming a Virtual Faith Community: Applying Past Data to New Ideas," *Faith Communities Today*, March 30, 2020, https://faithcommunitiestoday.org/becoming-a-virtual-faith-community-applying-past-data-to-new-ideas/.
6. Richard Rogers, *The E-Giving Guide for Every Church: Using Digital Tools to Grow Ministry* (Nashville, TN: Abingdon Press, 2016).
7. Cynthia D. Weems, "Online Giving Connects Ministry and Mission," *Leading Ideas E-Newsletter*, March 27, 2013, https://www.churchleadership.com/leading-ideas/online-giving-connects-ministry-and-mission/.

CHAPTER 8

1. J. Clif Christopher, *Not Your Parents' Offering Plate: A New Vision for Financial Stewardship* (Nashville, TN: Abingdon Press, 2008), 65–78.
2. Barbara Fullerton, "Growing Generosity: Identity as Stewards in the United Church of Canada" (doctoral thesis, Wesley Theological Seminary, 2009), 118.
3. David McAllister Wilson, "Why Clergy Personal Finances Matter," *Leading Ideas E-Newsletter*, October 21, 2015, https://www.churchleadership.com/leading-ideas/why-clergy-personal-finances-matter/.

CHAPTER 9

1. This phrase, commonly used in the healthcare world, is attributed to Sister Irene Krause, Daughters of Charity National Health Care System.
2. Keucher, *Remember the Future*, 34.
3. James Hudnut-Beumler, "Creating a Commonwealth: The History, Theology, and Ethics of Church Endowments," Presentation to the National Association of Endowed Presbyterian Churches, Chicago, IL, October 18, 1996, http://www.presbyterianendowment.org/node/41. He also applies the commonwealth concept to aspects of

congregational life in *Generous Saints: Congregations Rethinking Ethics and Money* (Lanham, MD: Rowman & Littlefield, 1999).

4. "Charitable Giving Statistics," *Nonprofits Source*, accessed July 12, 2020, https://nonprofitssource.com/online-giving-statistics/.

5. Christopher, *Not Your Parents' Offering Plate*, 72.

CHAPTER 10

1. Mary Parker Follett, *Freedom and Co-Ordination: Lectures in Business Organization* (London: Management Publication Trust, 1949), 55. While this phrase is associated with Follett (1868–1933) and her pioneering work in leadership, she says it was used by her contemporary Richard Cabot, a trained philosopher, lawyer, and medical doctor, who taught at Harvard.

2. King et al., *National Study of Congregations' Economic Practices*, 26. Their categories included one for "dues" at 6 percent, which is included here under missions where denominational giving is lodged.

CHAPTER 12

1. Quoted in Michael Durall, *Beyond the Offering Plate* (Nashville, TN: Abingdon Press, 2003), 141.

2. Jeffrey M. Jones, "Majority in U.S. Do Not Have a Will," *Gallup*, May 18, 2016, https://news.gallup.com/poll/191651/majority-not.aspx.

3. Brittany De Lea, "Get Ready for One of the Greatest Wealth Transfers in History," *New York Post*, March 13, 2018, https://nypost.com/2018/03/13/get-ready-for-one-of-the-greatest-wealth-transfers-in-history/.

4. CJ Orr and Devon McCann, "The $30 Trillion 'Great Wealth Transfer'—Some Planned Giving Tools to Help Nonprofits Benefit," *NonProfit Pro*, October 16, 2018, https://www.nonprofitpro.com/post/the-30-trillion-great-wealth-transfer-some-planned-giving-tools-to-help-nonprofits-benefit/.

CHAPTER 13

1. See Congregational Giving Profile (CGP), https://www.churchleadership.com/product/congregational-giving-profile-cgp-download/.

CHAPTER 15

1. Joe Daniels and Christie Latona, *Connecting for a Change: How to Engage People, Churches, and Partners to Inspire Hope in Your Community* (Nashville, TN: Abingdon Press, 2019), 38.

2. Ibid., 35.

CHAPTER 16

1. The Fresh Expression movement, which began in the Church of England, develops new and innovative expressions of church in places where people already gather or where there are common interests or affinities. See https://freshexpressionsus.org/ or Kenneth H. Carter and Audrey Warren, *Fresh Expressions: A New Kind of Methodist Church for People Not in Church* (Nashville, TN: Abingdon Press, 2017).

2. Hudnut-Beumler, *Generous Saints*, 74.

3. Ibid.

4. Mark Teasdale, *Go! How to Become a Great Commission Church* (Nashville, TN: General Board of Higher Education and Ministry, 2017), 87–89.

5. Mark DeYmaz, "The Coming Revolution in Church Economics" interview with Ann Michel, *Leading Ideas Talks*, podcast audio, episode 55, May 13, 2020.

6. Krin Van Tatenhove and Rob Mueller, *Neighborhood Church: Transforming Your Congregation into a Powerhouse for Mission* (Louisville, KY: Westminster John Knox Press, 2019), 75.

7. Ibid., 76.

8. Rosario Picardo, *Funding Ministry with Five Loaves and Two Fishes* (Nashville, TN: Abingdon, 2016), 46.

9. "Our Story," Shawnee Community Christian Church, accessed June 7, 2020, https://shawneecommunity.org/our-story/.

10. Mark DeYmaz, *Disruption: Repurposing the Church to Redeem the Community* (New York: Harper Collins, 2017), 115–123.

11. Waveney Ann Moore, "Christ United Methodist Selling Its Parking Lot in Hot Downtown St. Petersburg Market," *Tampa Bay Times*, December 20, 2017, https://www.tampabay.com/news/business/economicdevelopment/Christ-United-Methodist-selling-its-parking-lot-in-hot-downtown-St-Petersburg-market_163504218/.

12. Waveney Ann Moore, "From Tiny Downtown Parking Lot, St. Pete Church Blessed with Millions," *Tampa Bay Times*, March 4, 2020, https://www.tampabay.com/news/st-petersburg/2020/03/04/from-tiny-downtown-parking-lot-st-pete-church-blessed-with-millions/.

13. Jacqueline Jones-Smith, "Thinking Outside the Box: Finances for African American Churches Conference," presentation at Wesley Theological Seminary, Washington, DC, November 2, 2019.

14. Picardo, *Funding Ministry with Five Loaves and Two Fishes*, 35–36.

15. Ibid., 47–49.

16. Eddy Hall, Ray Bowman, and J. Skipp Machmer, *The More-with-Less Church: Maximize Your Money, Space, Time, and People to Multiply Ministry Impact* (Grand Rapids, MI: Baker Books, 2014).

17. Teasdale, *Go! How to Become a Great Commission Church*, 87.

18. Tatenhove and Mueller, *Neighborhood Church*, 75–76.

CHAPTER 17

1. King et al., *National Study of Congregations' Economic Practices*, 15.

2. Hudnut-Beumler, *Generous Saint*, 73.

3. Keucher, *Remember the Future*, 115–123.

4. Two helpful discussions of how to calculate costs that inform our summary are Hudnut-Beumler, *Generous Saints*, 73–76 and Keucher, *Remember the Future*, 123–126.

5. Often there are no tax implications, but you need to refer to the IRS publication "Tax Guide for Churches and Religious Organizations" available at the Internal Revenue Service website. If the nature or size of the arrangement does involve tax liability, remember that using the language of "donation" does not change your liability.

CHAPTER 18

1. Sidney S. Williams, Jr., *Fishing Differently: Ministry Formation in the Marketplace* (Apopka, FL: Certa Publishing, 2018), 11–12.

2. Joy Skjegstad, "Are Grants the Answer?" *Faith and Leadership*, July 6, 2009, https://faithandleadership.com/are-grants-answer?utm_source=albanweekly&utm_medium=content&utm_campaign=faithleadership.

3. Williams, *Fishing Differently*, 54–55.

4. Sarah Perry, "Morganton: Open Hearts Bakery," *Our State* magazine, March 28, 2013, https://www.ourstate.com/open-hearts-bakery-morganton/.

5. Picardo, *Funding Ministry with Five Loaves and Two Fishes*, 51.

6. U.S. Census Bureau, "New Census Data Show Differences Between Urban and Rural Populations," December 8, 2016, Release number CB16–210, https://www.census.gov/newsroom/press-releases/2016/cb16-210.html.

7. Amy Symens Smith and Edward Trevelyan, "In Some States, More Than Half of Older Residents Live in Rural Areas," October 22, 2019, https://www.census.gov/library/stories/2019/10/older-population-in-rural-america.html.

8. An analysis by the Lewis Center for Church Leadership of United Methodist congregational assets for 2016 showed that net assets per worshiper increased as attendance became smaller. Net assets for churches averaging twenty-five or fewer in worship were $29,216 per worshiper compared to $13,612 for churches averaging 1,000 or more in worship. When limited to "non-property assets" (endowments, special funds beyond the operating budget, or other nonproperty assets), these assets represented on average 160 percent of church operating expenditures in churches with twenty-five or fewer in worship, while such assets represented only 71 percent in churches averaging 1,000 or more in worship. The median comparison is closer, 55 percent for the smaller group and 46 percent for the larger group.

9. G. Jeffrey MacDonald, *Part-Time Is Plenty: Thriving without Full-time Clergy* (Louisville, KY: Westminster John Knox Press, 2020), 61.

10. Ibid.

11. National Congregations Study, Cumulative Dataset, 2012, http://www.thearda.com/ConQS/qs_295.asp.

12. Lee Ann M. Pomrenke, "Closing a Congregation as an Act of Faithfulness," *Leading Ideas* E-Newsletter, February 7, 2018, https://www.churchleadership.com/leading-ideas/closing-a-congregation-as-an-act-of-faithfulness/.

13. Ibid.

CHAPTER 19

1. Smith, Emerson, and Snell developed a framework using two proto-typical categories of churches, "Pay-the-Bills Churches" and "Live-the-Vision Churches." *Passing the Plate*, 128–138.

2. Charles R. Lane, *Ask, Thank, Tell: Improving Stewardship Ministry in Your Congregation* (Minneapolis, MN: Augsburg Fortress, 2006), 95.

3. See Episcopal Diocese of West Texas, "Year-Round Stewardship Calendar," https://www.dwtx.org/departments/stewardship/year-round-stewardship/ and "Year-round Planning Calendar for Growing Stewards in Your Congregation," https://download.elca.org/ELCA%20Resource%20Repository/Year_round_Planning_Calendar_for_Growing_Stewa.pdf.

4. Satterlee, *Preaching and Stewardship*, 22–23.

CHAPTER 20

1. Lovett H. Weems, Jr., *Church Leadership: Vision, Team, Culture, and Integrity*, rev. ed. (Nashville, TN: Abingdon Press, 2010).

2. Bernice Anderson Poole, *Mary McLeod Bethune: Educator* (Los Angeles, CA: Melrose Square, 1994), 153.

3. John Wesley, *The Letters of the Rev. John Wesley, A.M.*, Vol. 5, edited by John Telford (London: Epworth Press, 1931), 108–109.

4. John Wesley, "An Earnest Appeal to Men of Reason and Religion," in *The Works of John Wesley*, Vol. 11, edited by Gerald R. Cragg (Nashville, TN: Abingdon Press, 1989), 87–88.

5. Alexis de Tocqueville, *Democracy in America* (New York: Harper Perennial Modern Classics, 2006), 536.

Subject Index

Scripture Index